# The Noble Spa

## A Comedy

W. Somerset Maugham

Adapted from
the French of Grenet-Dancourt

*Samuel French – London*
*New York – Sydney – Toronto – Hollywood*

---

### For Amateur Production Enquiries

#### United Kingdom and World excluding north america
plays@SamuelFrench-London.co.uk
020 7255 4302/01

Each title is subject to availability from Samuel French,
depending upon country of performance.

---

# The Noble Spaniard

By W. SOMERSET MAUGHAM (adapted from the French of *Grenet-Dancourt*).
The play was first produced at the New Royalty Theatre, London, on
Saturday, 20th March, 1909, with the following cast :—

| | |
|---|---|
| LADY PROUDFOOT .. .. .. .. .. | *Miss Fanny Brough* |
| MR. JUSTICE PROUDFOOT (her husband) .. .. | *Mr. E. Lyall Swete* |
| MARION NAIRNE (a young widow) .. .. | *Miss Kate Cutler* |
| LUCY (her sister) .. .. .. .. .. | *Miss Anne Cleaver* |
| MARY JANE (a maid).. .. .. .. .. | *Miss Joy Chatwyn* |
| CAPTAIN CHALFORD .. .. .. .. .. | *Mr. Athol Stewart* |
| COUNT DE MORET (a Frenchman).. .. .. | *Mr. Leon M. Lion* |
| COUNTESS DE MORET (his English wife) .. .. | *Miss Vane Featherston* |
| THE DUKE OF HERMANOS (a Spaniard) .. .. | *Mr. Charles Hawtrey* |

*The action of the play takes place in a villa at Boulogne in the
year 1850*

### ACT I
A summer morning.

### ACT II
The same afternoon.

### ACT III
Late the same evening.

# INTRODUCTION

*Of the original of this production in 1909 the famous A. B. Walkley, of "The Times", wrote an anonymous criticism which still serves as an admirable description, and one which producers to-day might well find useful:*

Only a Diogenes Teufelsdröckh could do justice to the clothes-philosophy of "The Noble Spaniard". Why does an elderly Englishwoman staying at Boulogne in 1850 spout Byron and talk of being thrown in a sack into the Bosphorus? You feel sure, instinctively, rather than by any process of strict reasoning, that the explanation is to be found in her costume. Lady Proudfoot wears (over a crinoline, pantaloons, white stockings, and sandals) a red, plaid skirt bunched and flounced and a muslin breakfast jacket, or else a green jacket of moiré antique, or else a yellow, plaid dress and a turban of gold tissue. How could you expect her, so clothed, to be anything else than Byronic and given to talking of her "boo-som"?

Mrs. Nairne wears embroidered flounces, a long pointed bodice of China silk, a wreath of roses and ringlets. What else could you expect from a pretty widow, so attired, than a perpetual languishing for a romantic suitor, with raven locks and whiskers? The romantic black-whiskered gentleman soon presents himself, and presses his suit with inconvenient fervour—wearing very tight trousers, cape and sombrero. He is Duke of Hermanos, a grandee of Spain, and entitled to wear his hat in the presence of the king: but the king doesn't happen to be there, so he doffs his hat to the queen of his heart, the bewitching, crinolined, ringleted Mrs. Nairne. To cool his ardour the lady hints at a husband, but the suggestion only fans the Spaniard's flame. He is devoured by a fatal passion, and "passion", he declares, "purifies everything—even respectability". What is more, he will seek out this husband and have his blood. Several of the others profess a craving for the "blood" of their enemies, in order that they may "wallow in it". Oh, Byron! Oh, crinolines!

All the fun of the farce (for those who have no clothes-philosophy) comes from the Spaniard's efforts to find his beloved's husband and his successive provocations, of every man he meets in her company, to mortal combat. As his first victim happens to be Mr. Justice Proudfoot, who is misled as to the particular object of the Spaniard's affections through the mis-delivery of a bouquet (an authentically stiff, ugly Victorian nosegay), the virtue of the poor lady in the green and moiré antique is soon called in question. Dismayed by visions of a sack and the Bosphorus she protests that she is "pure", but is, nevertheless, a good deal chagrined when the Byronic gentleman treats her as a mother. "You may be a grandee of Spain," she says witheringly, "but you are not one of nature's noblemen."

Then there is a certain captain of Heavy Dragoons in stock, rolled collar, and frogged surtout, who prodigiously admires his sweetheart, Miss Lucy (a delicious little minx in a poke-bonnet), when she sings verses by Mrs. Hemans to excruciatingly Victorian music, and addresses her as "ma'am" when out of temper. In due course the captain gets challenged by the Spaniard, and nothing delights him more than the chance of a duel with a "wretched foreigner". A French gentleman also receives the Spaniard's challenge and, as the maid announces, "please mum", that the grandee is now sitting in the back garden surrounded by swords and pistols, there is every prospect of our Byronically wallowing in blood. But, of course, the teasing little widow relents in the nick of time, and is pressed to the Spaniard's "boo-som".

Miss Kate Cutler makes a delightful Victorian roguey-poguey in ringlets. The shy little puss has only one idea—matrimony—in her pretty head, prefers in a man a combination of whiskers and romantic devotion, is quite modest, but has no insuperable objection to being kissed (as, indeed, she is by the grandee, with quite Andalusian rapture), and might have walked straight out of one of Trollope's earlier novels. It is not every actress who can be retrospectively Victorian; Miss Cutler realizes for us the very type of woman of the crinoline-and-ringlets period. Miss Fanny Brough as Lady Proudfoot strikes a deeper note, deep as her Byron and her Bosphorus; but, then, she has always been a mistress of the tragi-comic and of the "grand grotesque of farce". Miss Anne Cleaver and Mr. Athol Stewart and Mr. Lyall Swete as sweetheart, captain and Judge are all properly and drolly Victorian. As the Spaniard, Mr. Hawtrey, who evidently has not yet recovered full strength after his recent illness, was not on Saturday night quite so volcanic as his part. A little more fire, and all will be well. Meanwhile, the tall and bell-shaped "topper" which supersedes his sombrero in the last act is a triumph of Victorian "reconstitution". So, by the way, is every detail of wallpaper, pictures and furniture. The sarcophagus-shaped sofa and the wax-fruits under a glass shade give us especial joy.

*From "The Times" of March 22nd, 1909, reprinted by kind permission.*

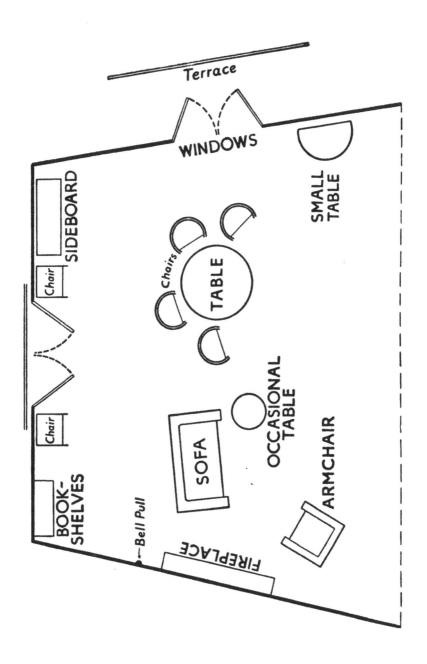

Stage plan as described in the opening text.

# THE NOBLE SPANIARD

## ACT ONE

SCENE: *The dining-room of the Proudfoots' villa, Boulogne, in 1850. Morning.*
*Up stage* C. *magnificent double-doors (simply pining for stylish entrances), over stage* R. *a stately fireplace, and* L., *windows opening out on to a garden-terrace connecting with other parts of the house. Between the windows and the* C. *stage is a large, round folding-table, set about with four chairs (all angled toward the audience). Jutting out from the fireplace is a sofa (with an occasional table at its head) and below it,* D.S.R., *a low armchair, angled toward the top* L. *corner of the stage. There are other pleasing pieces of furniture, of course, and an abundance of flowers.*

> *When the curtain rises,* PROUDFOOT *is seated at the head of the breakfast table,* LADY PROUDFOOT *to his* R., MARION *to his* L., *and* LUCY *a little lower down the table.*

> PROUDFOOT *is a pompous man of* 55, *good-natured and, as becomes a judge, fond of a joke. Fully dressed, except for his jacket, he wears a dressing gown. His wife is ten years younger, a stout woman, obviously painted and much over-dressed.* MARION *is a young widow, fascinating and handsome.* LUCY *is* 18.

LADY PROUDFOOT (*proffering a cup*). May I have some more sugar?

PROUDFOOT (*looking over his paper*). You've already had three lumps, Matilda.

LADY PROUDFOOT. I want four, Sebastian.

MARION (*dropping another lump in the cup*). Lady Proudfoot likes her coffee sweet.

LADY PROUDFOOT. Thank you. I always did—even when I was a child.

PROUDFOOT. It must be obvious to the meanest intelligence that you're a child no longer, Matilda.

LADY PROUDFOOT (*stirring, with an air*). My tastes haven't altered, Sebastian.

PROUDFOOT. Your figure has, my dear.

LUCY. Law! you do tease your wife, Judge.

PROUDFOOT (*taking up his cup*). It keeps her up to the mark.

MARION (*smiling*). I think you're a horrid husband. I'm glad I'm not married to you.

LADY PROUDFOOT (*affectionately*). I don't mind what he says, my dear. (*To* PROUDFOOT.) Do I, dearest? (*Gives him a friendly but rather violent tap.*)

    (PROUDFOOT *has just put his cup up to his mouth, and some of the contents are spilt.*)

PROUDFOOT. Now you've spilt my coffee, Matilda. I dislike these foreign breakfasts quite enough as it is without having them spilt all over my clothes.

LADY PROUDFOOT (*rising, and dabbing with a napkin*). Let me dry it for you, darling.

PROUDFOOT (*cup in one hand, newspaper in the other: helpless*). Don't fuss me about, Matilda. I don't like it.

    (LUCY *rises and helps.*)

MARION. You're a very lucky man to have a wife who spoils you so much.

LADY PROUDFOOT (*straightening his necktie*). I'm like a mother to him.

PROUDFOOT. I often wonder that I'm not taken for your son, Matilda.

LADY PROUDFOOT (*standing back to survey her work*). Your age makes any such mistake improbable.

PROUDFOOT. I don't know so much about that. Let me see; you were born in the year . . .

LADY PROUDFOOT (*with asperity, sitting*). I cannot bear this passion of yours for telling everyone how old I am. In point of fact, a woman is only as old as she looks.

PROUDFOOT (*looking at his wife*). I don't know that that's always an advantage.

LADY PROUDFOOT. Sebastian, I shall burst into tears.

PROUDFOOT. Anything but that, Matilda.

LADY PROUDFOOT. Then give me a kiss.

PROUDFOOT. These little jokes of mine always get me into trouble. (*Kisses her hand.*) There, will that do?

LADY PROUDFOOT. You usen't to kiss me like that when first we were married. Don't you remember, Sebastian, how you used to press me to your bosom?

PROUDFOOT. Matilda, don't be immodest. (*Quickly, to* LUCY, *and rising.*) Won't you sing us a little song, Lucy, my dear?

LUCY (*with a little laugh*). We've come to the seaside to enjoy ourselves. (*Moves to occasional table by sofa and takes up tapestry.*)

PROUDFOOT. That's right, my dear. That's right. The young should always be doing something.

(LUCY *begins to work, sitting in armchair* D.S.R.)

MARION (*with a little smile*). It makes the idleness of the middle-aged so much more enjoyable.

(PROUDFOOT *moves to fireplace* R.)

LADY PROUDFOOT (*continuing to breakfast, regardless*). Have you done, dear?

PROUDFOOT. Done in a manner of speaking. I have eaten two rolls and had three cups of coffee, the last of which you precipitated upon my dressing-gown. But I have momentarily appeased the pangs of hunger. Let us, however, turn to a pleasanter topic of conversation. (*To* MARION.) I think it was a capital idea for you and Lucy to spend your summer with us here.

MARION (*moving to sofa,* R.). It was very kind of you to have us. It would have been impossible for us to come here by ourselves.

LADY PROUDFOOT (*turning in her chair*). My dear, you're a widow and therefore quite fit to chaperon your sister

MARION (*sitting on sofa*). Do you think it is very safe to be a young widow with a rather large fortune?

LUCY. If it's unsafe, why don't you marry again?

PROUDFOOT. That girl has a legal mind. There is no character-istic, my dear Matilda, which has had greater weight in my advancement to the position which I now enjoy than that of seizing upon the obvious with unerring accuracy. (*To* MARION.) Why don't you marry again?

MARION. Can you ask me, when you know how desperately wretched I was with my first husband?

PROUDFOOT. Mr. Nairne had his faults, but he redeemed them by breaking his neck within two years of your marriage and leaving you exceedingly well provided for.

LADY PROUDFOOT. He was an iceberg. He had no passion.

PROUDFOOT. My dear, I deplore this tendency of yours to employ a word which is not used in refined circles.

MARION. I shouldn't have minded his not liking me very much if only he hadn't liked his gin and water more.

LADY PROUDFOOT. You should have married a man like Sebastian. A man of fire.

PROUDFOOT. Matilda, I must request you to preserve the re-spect due to a judge of the Queen's Bench.

LUCY. I should have thought, if you weren't happy with your first husband, it was all the more reason to try a second.

LADY PROUDFOOT. I'm sure I couldn't live without a man. Could I, Sebastian?

PROUDFOOT. I don't know, my dear. I've never thought it necessary to consider the matter.

MARION. There are advantages in being a widow. You can do what you like, see whom you will, and go where you choose. I've come here to divert myself. Please don't remind me that I ever had a husband.

LUCY. I don't know why you're so obstinate. You're young and charming and nice. And what is the use of it all if you're not going to make someone else happy?

LADY PROUDFOOT. If I were a widow, I wouldn't hesitate for a moment.

PROUDFOOT. I must beg you to remember that I'm still alive, Matilda. I don't at all like these speculations as to your behaviour on my decease. I should expect you to shave your head and go into a nunnery. And I may as well tell you that though I have left you handsomely provided for, it is only *dum casta et sola*—while you are a widow—(*pause*) and properly conducted.

LUCY. Well, Marion?

MARION. You're a deceitful little wretch and you're not thinking of me for a moment. The only reason you want me to marry is that you're engaged to Captain Chalford. There's no logic in that.

LUCY. Oh, Marion, how can you?

PROUDFOOT. Upon my soul, you're blushing, Lucy.

LUCY. What nonsense!

PROUDFOOT. Now you're the colour of a peony.

LUCY. You're a perfect tease, and I hate you.

LADY PROUDFOOT. My dear, don't be ashamed of it. Of course, you're in love and love is the most beautiful thing in the world. It's the only thing in the world worth living for. And Captain Chalford has the most adorable whiskers.

PROUDFOOT. I shall not bring you to a French watering-place a second time, Matilda. It has a most alarming effect on you.

LADY PROUDFOOT. Are you very fond of the Captain?

LUCY. I'm immoderately in love with him . . . and he simply dotes on me.

PROUDFOOT. Dear me, how do you know that?

LUCY. He tells me so, all day long.

LADY PROUDFOOT. Lucky child! She's the very image of me at eighteen.

PROUDFOOT. You've changed, Matilda. Even the most unprejudiced observer couldn't help saying you've changed.

(*Doors* B.S. *open and* MARY JANE, *the maid, comes in.*)

MARY. Captain Chalford, my lady.

(CAPTAIN CHALFORD *enters. He is very gallant and very military.* MARY JANE *closes doors behind him.*)

CHALFORD (*advancing and bowing*). Ladies, I kiss your hands; Mr. Justice Proudfoot, your obedient servant.

PROUDFOOT. I'm pleased to see you, sir.

LUCY. It's nice of you to come so early.

PROUDFOOT. Very. If you'd arrived a little earlier you'd have found us in bed.

CHALFORD. I haven't an idea what o'clock it is. I only know that it seems a century since last I saw my Lucy.

MARION. Won't you have some breakfast?

CHALFORD. No, thank you. I've already had it.

LADY PROUDFOOT. Besides, when one's in love one never has an appetite.

PROUDFOOT. Matilda, I still remember the hearty meals you ate when we were engaged.

LADY PROUDFOOT. Oh, Sebastian, you have a soul dead to romance.

CHALFORD. I came to ask if you wouldn't care for a picnic to-day.

LADY PROUDFOOT (*folding her napkin at last*). I dote on picnics.

PROUDFOOT. I cannot see the pleasure of eating one's dinner on the grass, which is probably damp, when Providence has placed within one's reach chairs and a table and the other resources of civilisation.

(MARY JANE *enters to announce:*)

MARY. Please, my lady, the Count and Countess de Moret.

(CAPTAIN CHALFORD *moves over* R., *to behind sofa. Enter* COUNT *and* COUNTESS DE MORET. MARY JANE *goes out, closing doors.*)

MARION (*rising and advancing*). How do you do?

(*General greeting.*)

How early you are.

COUNT (C.S.). I've the *diligence* to catch. I have ze shopping to do for my wife.

COUNTESS. It's only by making him do all my shopping that I keep him away from the gaming tables.

> (COUNTESS *and* LADY PROUDFOOT *stand together by table*, L.)

LUCY. I don't know where you're going, but you must get me some chocolates.

COUNT. *Certainement.* (*To* MARION, *gallantly.*) And what can I bring you, *belle dame?*

MARION. Nothing, thanks.

COUNT (*stroking his whiskers in a killing way*). I wish I could do something for you. I would do anything. Upon my soul. Upon my soul.

MARION (*gaily to* COUNTESS). Kate, I believe your husband is making love to me.

COUNTESS. I congratulate you. He never does it to me.

LADY PROUDFOOT. How like Sebastian.

> (*They laugh together.*)

COUNT. My dear Kate. I promise you . . .

COUNTESS. Oh, don't apologise, *mon cher.* In the first place, I don't in the least want you to make love to me, and in the second, I'm not at all jealous.

MARION. One can never be too careful with a good-looking husband.

LADY PROUDFOOT. Those are my sentiments.

COUNT. You are too good, madam. You are too good.

COUNTESS. I feel quite safe with mine.

LUCY (*moving to sofa, to* CHALFORD). I'm dreadfully jealous. And if you ever flirt with anyone else . . .

CHALFORD (*moves round sofa to join* LUCY). As if I should, Lucy.

LADY PROUDFOOT. There, Sebastian, there's an example for you.

PROUDFOOT. The Captain hasn't been married for seven and twenty years.

COUNTESS (*to* COUNT). Now you must go, or you'll miss the *diligence* and you'll never get back.

COUNT. Observe how my wife drives me away from her side. Good-bye, then, for the present, ladies.

LUCY. Take care you are not late for the ball to-night.

PROUDFOOT. Are we going to a ball?

LUCY. You hadn't forgotten, had you?

(COUNT *bows and goes out, leaving doors open.*)

MARION. Now I think you'd all better go and catch some shrimps for tea.

PROUDFOOT. Will you explain to me, my dear Marion, why one should put oneself to considerable inconvenience in order to catch a few uncooked shrimps which one can buy in a shop all ready to eat?

LADY PROUDFOOT. I love paddling. It's so French.

PROUDFOOT (*moving* C., *to his wife*). I do not approve of this passion you have, Matilda, for displaying your lower extremities to the admiring gaze of foreigners.

MARION. Lady Proudfoot has a very neat ankle, and of course she wants to show it.

PROUDFOOT. You may not be aware of the fact, Marion, but I flatter myself that I have no need to be ashamed of the corresponding portions of my anatomy.

MARION. Then you must certainly go shrimping, too.

LUCY. Will *you* come, Adolphus? (*Taking his hand.*)

CHALFORD. With you I will go anywhere.

LADY PROUDFOOT. Law! what a perfect gentleman. Will you come, Sebastian?

PROUDFOOT. The lamb is ready for the slaughter, Matilda. (*Taking her hand.*)

(*Led by* PROUDFOOT, *they go out, chatting. Doors are closed.* MARION *and* COUNTESS *remain.*)

MARION (*sitting on sofa*). They've been trying to persuade me to marry again.

COUNTESS (C.S.). Why don't you? It must be very dull to be a widow.

MARION. I don't want again to lead the horrid life I did with Jack.

COUNTESS. It's true your first choice was not lucky but that's no reason why your second shouldn't be.

MARION. I prefer to run no risks. Ah, my dear, if we only knew before marriage what we know afterwards ...

COUNTESS (*interrupting*). We should be even more determined to marry than we are now. My dear, you're talking nonsense. Of course you must marry again.

MARION. Then find me a really nice man, with a sound heart and good digestion, amusing and kind and tolerant ...

COUNTESS (*sinking on arm of sofa, looking toward window*, L.). You're asking a good deal.

MARION. A man who'll entertain me when I'm bored, leave me alone when I'm weary, and never lose his temper when I'm peevish.

COUNTESS. You'll marry him?

MARION. If you can assure me positively that he'll have all the good qualities after marriage that he seems to have before.

COUNTESS. I'm glad that you haven't stipulated that he should never repeat his stories, because that, my dear, you'll never find. (*Goes to window.*) Who on earth is that creature who looks as if he were doing sentry-go in front of the house?

MARION (*without looking up*). A dark man?

COUNTESS. Yes, a dark man.

MARION. Is he looking up at the windows?

COUNTESS. With all his eyes.

MARION. It's the noble Spaniard.

COUNTESS. And who is he, pray?

MARION. For goodness' sake, don't look. He'll think it's me.

COUNTESS (*coming back*). What on earth do you mean?

MARION. It's the usual man who follows women about at watering-places in the usual hope that some chance will

B

enable him to scrape the usual acquaintance. Haven't you seen him before?

COUNTESS. Never.

MARION. I've been here three weeks, and the noble stranger follows me like my shadow ; at a discreet and well-mannered distance, certainly, but he follows me all the same ; and in the most determined fashion, my dear.

COUNTESS. He's evidently a man of character.

MARION. And when I stay at home he wanders round and round the house like the sun. He's as regular as the tides and more persistent than a dun.

COUNTESS. Upon my word, it's very flattering. And has he never spoken to you?

MARION. Certainly not. But he looks at me—as if I were the most ravishing creature in the world.

COUNTESS (*quickly over to window*). How romantic! I should like to kiss my hand to him. He's really very good-looking.

MARION (*rising*). For heaven's sake, don't look out of the window. He'll think we're talking of him.

COUNTESS. Shall I draw the blind?

MARION. No. He'll think I'm afraid of him.

COUNTESS. Well, it's quite clear that he's desperately in love with you. Do you know anything about him?

MARION. I heard, quite by chance—

(COUNTESS *smiles incredulously, moving back to* MARION.)

quite by chance, that he was a Spanish nobleman ; very rich and very distinguished. And he certainly has the most charming blue eyes you ever saw.

COUNTESS. I think if a man followed me about for three weeks without saying a single word, I should be rather—interested.

MARION. But, you're married.

COUNTESS. Oh, my dear, do you suppose that because one's married one can't tell if a man has a straight nose or a crooked one.

MARION. I believe you're on the point of scolding me because I don't fall in love with him.

COUNTESS (*going back to window again, fascinated*). Well, it's quite obvious that you've turned his head completely.

MARION. You can't expect me to fall in love with everyone who falls in love with me.

COUNTESS. Hoity-toity! He's gone.

MARION. He'll come back.

COUNTESS. Oh! (*Looks at* MARION *with a smile of amusement, having seen from the window that the Spaniard is coming into the house.*) Well, I must leave you. I have ten thousand things to do. Good-bye.

MARION. But why are you in such a hurry?

COUNTESS. Good-bye. I'll come in again later and you shall tell me all about it.

MARION (*surprised*). About what?

(COUNTESS *opens doors and runs off with a laugh. At this moment the* SPANIARD'S *voice is heard off.*)

DUKE (*off*). I wish to see Mrs. Nairne.

MARION. Who on earth's that?

(SPANIARD *comes in, followed by* MARY JANE.)

MARY. What name shall I say, sir? I don't know whether you can see her.

MARION (*at fireplace*). Heavens, it's the noble Spaniard.

DUKE. Unless my eyes deceive, she stands before me.

MARION. I'm at home to no one, Mary Jane.

DUKE (*coming forward blandly*). Thank you, that will be much more convenient.

MARION. I meant my order to refer to you also, sir.

DUKE (*calmly*). Then you gave it at least three seconds too late.

MARION. You appear to have no false shame.

DUKE. That is a failing from which my birth amply protects me.

MARION (*trying not to smile*). I am almost disarmed by your extreme audacity.

DUKE. No one has ever accused me of faint heart, fair lady.

MARION. May I ask upon what business you come?

DUKE (*coolly*). Will you not dismiss your maid?

MARION (*helplessly*). You can go, Mary Jane.

> (MARY JANE *goes out, peering hard until doors are closed.*)

DUKE. Thank you.

MARION. I daresay it's better that we should have an explanation.

DUKE. Madam, your common sense is no less admirable than your personal appearance. (*With a wave of the hand.*) Pray be seated.

MARION (*overwhelmed*). Thank you. (*Sits on sofa, with dignity.*)

DUKE. First of all, you must allow me to tell you who I am.

MARION. I should have thought that completely unnecessary.

DUKE. Don Ferdinand Francisco Maria de Lomas y Oria, Duke of Hermanos, Marquis of Alcala, Count of Triana, Knight of the Golden Fleece, and a grandee of Spain, with the right to wear my hat in the presence of the King. (*Puts hat on his head.*) But since the King doesn't happen to be here, I take it off to the queen of my desires. (*Throws hat on chair* D.R.)

MARION (*with a bow*). Sir, you overwhelm me with confusion.

DUKE. Madam, for three weeks life has been impossible to me. I cannot eat, I cannot sleep. I can do nothing, absolutely nothing, but think of you.

MARION. I regret that I should unwittingly have to put you to considerable inconvenience, but I venture to suggest that you would find change of air an excellent remedy for your distemper.

DUKE. Madam, were I to say I loved you, I should grossly understate the fact. I adore the ground you tread on. I worship the air you breathe.

MARION. You really need not have taken the trouble to come and tell me.

DUKE. Why?

MARION. Because the ground I tread on and the air I breathe are not more indifferent to you than I am.

DUKE. Give yourself time, my dear lady, and you will dote upon me.

MARION. I see absolutely no reason to think so.

DUKE. I have no doubt of it. I am always right.

MARION. And is that all you had to say?

DUKE. By no means. Under the circumstances it is evidently necessary that you should become acquainted with me. Let us discuss the world in general, and ourselves in particular.

MARION. The prospect is alluring, but I have many more important things to do.

DUKE. Have you the heart to send away a man who comes to tell you that on your account for three weeks he has neither eaten nor slept.

MARION. May I offer you some coffee? I'm afraid it's cold, but the buns are very nice.

DUKE. It is not very nice buns my soul yearns for, madam— but love.

MARION. That I certainly can't offer you . . . After all, it's too absurd. I don't know who you are, nor where you come from.

DUKE. I thought I told you. Don Ferdinand Francisco Maria de Lomas y Oria.

MARION. Duke of Hermanos and Marquis of Alcala. I remember perfectly.

DUKE. With the right to wear my hat in the presence of the King.

MARION. And as you justly remarked, the King doesn't happen to be here. But that's really no reason why you should come here and make me declarations of undying affection. The world would be a very inconvenient place to live in if anyone could walk in at the front door and say: "I love you. Will you be mine?" You really didn't think I was going to fall into your arms, and answer: "By all means".

DUKE. I did, indeed.

MARION. Well, you were mistaken, so there's an end of it. Now I must beg you to take your departure.

DUKE. I cannot. I can no longer. Before I had spoken to you I loved you to the verge of madness, but now that I have heard the delightful sound of your voice, it is no longer love I feel—it's rapture, passion, ecstasy.

MARION. Very well, if you refuse to take your leave, I must take mine. (*Rises, curtsies, goes towards the door* U.C.)

DUKE (*turning* U.S., *as* MARION *moves*). It is better so. The sight of a corpse is naturally unpleasing to a woman of sentiment.

MARION (*stopping at door*). May I inquire whose corpse you're talking about?

DUKE. My own.

MARION (*advancing to* C., *with some concern*). What do you mean?

DUKE. I mean that, since I cannot live by your side, I cannot live at all. Farewell, madam, I beg you to retire.

MARION. If you can do it briefly, would you have the goodness to explain?

DUKE. In five minutes you may come back to take away the remains of him who will have died with your name on his lips. . .

MARION. D'you mean to say you want to kill yourself? But I won't have it on any account.

DUKE (*radiant*). Blessed goddess, you call me back to life.

MARION. Not at all. I call you back to common-sense. You must be as mad as a hatter.

DUKE. Why a hatter?

MARION. In England hatters and March hares are peculiarly liable to insanity. Now, for heaven's sake, be reasonable. Promise me that you won't do anything rash—at all events, not here. You know, we've only taken this villa for the summer. The landlord might not like it.

DUKE. I will spare myself, on one condition.

MARION. And what is that?

DUKE. That you won't be angry with me for having thrust myself upon you.

MARION. No, I won't be angry.

DUKE. Then we're the best of friends, aren't we?

MARION. I don't know that we've got as far as that.

DUKE. And you will allow me to come and see you again?

MARION. Oh no, I can't possibly do that.

DUKE. Sometimes? What beautiful teeth you have. You should smile always.

MARION. Not even sometimes.

DUKE. Every day? How graceful your hand is. It's like some delicate flower in spring.

MARION (*aside, meditatively*). How on earth am I to get rid of him? (*Getting an idea.*) Oh! I'm afraid I can't ask you to come here again. You see, I'm not—my own mistress.

DUKE. I beg your pardon?

MARION. There's my husband to consider.

DUKE (*dumbfounded*). Your husband? You don't mean to say you're married?

MARION. Of course.

DUKE. Are you quite sure?

MARION. It's not the kind of thing one's likely to be mistaken about.

DUKE. They told me you were a widow.

MARION. How very strange . . . and how improbable!

(DUKE *walks up and down in agitation, while she watches him with a smile.*)

DUKE (*stopping suddenly, with resolution*). Well, I don't care— what you call—a damn . . .

MARION (*displaying shock superbly*). I beg your pardon?

DUKE (*on his knees*). Wife or widow, you're equally adorable. And I adore you.

MARION (*withdrawing, magnificently*). You must have taken leave of your senses.

DUKE. Love is above these gross and sordid details. And mine is so profound and so sincere that it cannot fail to move you.

MARION. There is still my husband to consider!

DUKE (*rising*). We will deceive him.

MARION. Never! Marion Nairne will never do anything that could bring a blush of shame to the cheek of her maternal grandmother.

DUKE. You do not know me yet. I have a soul of fire.

MARION. I am a pattern of respectability.

DUKE. Love purifies all things—even respectability—Marion—Marion.

MARION. Do you know my name?

DUKE. Of course I know your name. I repeat it to myself a thousand times a day. I have carved it upon every tree in the vicinity.

MARION. I think you've taken a great liberty.

DUKE. Look at the first oak you come across, and you will see your name and mine, Marion and Ferdinand, enclosed in a heart and transfixed by the arrow of love. Marion, I love you.

MARION. Nonsense! If you loved me, you'd think a little less of yourself, and a little more of me. My husband's a monster of jealousy, and if he finds you here—he'll kill us both.

DUKE. I fear not death.

MARION. Yes, but I do.

DUKE. Dear heart, I would not cause you one moment's uneasiness.

MARION (*gives him his hat*). Then, for goodness' sake, go away.

DUKE. I have had too much trouble in getting here. (*Sits on sofa.*) I shall remain.

MARION. You're making yourself quite at home. (*Suddenly gets an idea.*) Ah, now I have it! (*Goes to window aloud.*) Gracious heavens! I'm lost!

DUKE (*springing to his feet*). What is it?

MARION (*tragically*). My husband! For heaven's sake, go, go, go!

DUKE. A Spaniard never goes. I shall remain. (*Swings feet on to sofa.*)

MARION. Then—then I shall throw myself out of the window.

DUKE (*terrified, rising*). Marion, not that!

MARION (*drooping*). I could not bear the shame.

DUKE. Marion, I'll go. But I love you more than ever.

MARION (*moving to c.*). I don't care two straws so long as you make haste. And never let me see your face again.

DUKE. Give me that flower you are wearing in your dress.

MARION. No.

DUKE. Let me kiss the tips of your dainty fingers?

MARION (*giving him her hand*). It is cruel to take advantage of my agitation.

DUKE. Now give me that flower.

MARION (*giving it to him*). Go, go, go!

DUKE. I will keep this next to my heart for ever. *Hasta la vista!* (*Exit, with style, through windows, L.*)

MARION (*with a laugh*). Thank heaven! Oh, I thought I never should get rid of him. Now he thinks I'm married I suppose he'll leave me in peace. (*Goes to window.*) He is not ill-favoured. I rather like the way he walks.

(*Doors open, B.S., and LUCY and CHALFORD enter. LUCY is supporting CHALFORD.*)

Good gracious! What is the matter?

LUCY. Quick, Marion! Get a chair! A chair!

(CHALFORD *falls fainting on the sofa.* LUCY *moves behind sofa, bending over.*)

MARION. Oh, he's fainting. What shall we do? Where are my salts?

LUCY. Oh, do be quick.

MARION (*taking a small bottle from mantelpiece*). Ah, here they are. (*To* CHALFORD, *kneeling before him.*) Take a long breath.

CHALFORD. Thank you. Now I'm better.

MARION (*anxiously*). What is the matter with you?

CHALFORD (*recovering*). Nothing's the matter with me. It's Lucy.

LUCY. It was stupid of me. I slipped on a rock, and it gave the poor Captain such a turn that I had to bring him home.

CHALFORD. I was more agitated than when, single-handed, I cut down seventeen of the enemy on the banks of the Irrawaddy.

LUCY. We know your lion heart, Adolphus.

CHALFORD. Oh, Lucy, tell me that you're not hurt!

LUCY. Not a bit. I only grazed my shin.

CHALFORD. Are you sure that you won't be disfigured? Lucy, whatever happens, nothing shall alter my feelings towards you.

LUCY. Adolphus!

CHALFORD. Lucy!

MARION (*to* LUCY). Hadn't you better go to your room and have it seen to?

LUCY. I will—— (*She goes out* U.S.)

CHALFORD. I shall venture to enquire later on about my Lucy's health. But I must go for a turn. (CHALFORD *goes out,* U.S.)

MARION. Very well. So do. How lucky I got rid of the Spaniard before they came. Fortunately, I shall never see him again.

(*Turns round to find herself face to face with the* DUKE— *who has come back through windows,* L.)

DUKE. Your obedient servant, madam.

MARION (*with a cry*). Oh, how you frightened me!

DUKE. That is not the effect which I desired to create upon you.

MARION. I do hate people who jump up at odd moments like a Jack-in-the-box. Besides, how can you come here when you know that my husband's returned?

DUKE. It is precisely that which brings me. I have been medi-
tating. When I thought you were a widow I loved you.
But now that I know you are married, I love you to distraction. I tell you I have a soul of fire. What do you think
I care for the paltry impediments of the marriage knot?

MARION. I suppose you do know what you're talking about?

DUKE. You have a husband? Very good. He has come back.
Capital. Beg him to favour me with his presence.

MARION. My poor friend, you must be a perfect lunatic.

DUKE. Not at all. I'm particularly sane.

MARION. And why do you want to see my husband?

DUKE. Obviously there are but two alternatives. He loves you,
or he loves you not. If he doesn't, he will surrender his
claims without difficulty.

MARION. He simply dotes on me.

DUKE. I'm sorry for that. But in that case, of course he'll
understand that there is no room on this earth for both of us.

MARION. You're not proposing to assassinate my lawful
husband?

DUKE. I regret the painful necessity, but I can think of no other
course . . . I have never, never loved a woman as I love you;
I will never, never consent to share your heart with another.

MARION. It sounds so reasonable that I feel quite giddy.

DUKE. I beg you to send for your husband without delay.

MARION. But surely I am of some importance in this matter?

DUKE. Lady, I worship the very ground you tread on.

MARION. I have already explained to you clearly that the
ground you tread on is distressingly indifferent to me.

DUKE. You do not love me yet; but you will, you will, you
will.

MARION. But I tell you I won't, I won't, I won't.

DUKE. Madam, produce this man who dares to stand between
us.

MARION. Don't be so foolish. I shall do nothing of the sort.

DUKE. Then I must seek him out for myself.

MARION (*pulls bell-cord by fireplace*). I refuse to have anything more to do with you. You're too ridiculous.

DUKE. But dearest heart . . .

(MARY JANE *appears.*)

MARION. Show this gentleman the door. (*Bows to* DUKE.) Sir, I wish you a very good morning. (*Exit, through windows,* L.)

DUKE. I will not budge one inch till I have seen him!

MARY. If you please, sir.

DUKE. Ah, the maid. My dear, do you know what love is?

MARY (*with a curtsey*). I've lived in the very best families, my lord.

DUKE. You're a good girl. I want you to do something for me. I wonder if a louis would be of any use to you?

MARY. Thank you for nothing. I'm not one of that sort. If you don't mind what you are about, I shall tell the master. (*She goes to doors,* U.S.)

DUKE. Now you come to the point. Where is your master?

MARY. You had better take care. (*Turns away and sees* PROUD-FOOT *coming.*) He's just coming in.

DUKE. At last!

(PROUDFOOT *enters* U.S., *shrimping net in hand, his trousers turned up, with bare feet. He is holding his boots.*)

PROUDFOOT (*giving her the net*). Remove this bauble, Mary Jane.

MARY. Very good, sir. This gentleman wishes to speak to you, sir.

PROUDFOOT. Very well. You may withdraw.

(MARY *goes out.*)

DUKE (*looking at* PROUDFOOT). So that is the husband!

PROUDFOOT (*waving him to a chair*). Pray sit down. May I ask whom I have the honour of addressing?

DUKE (*with a flourish*).  Don Ferdinand Francisco Maria de Lomas y Oria, Duke of Hermanos, Marquis of Alcala, Knight of the Golden Fleece and a grandee of Spain, with the right to wear my hat in the presence of the King. (*Puts on hat.*)

PROUDFOOT (*taken aback, puts his on*).  Not at all.  Not at all.

DUKE.  But since the King doesn't happen to be here . . . (*Removes his hat.*)

PROUDFOOT (*removes hat—aside*).  This is a very odd person.  I wonder what he wants.

DUKE.  Sit, let us waste no time on idle preliminaries.

PROUDFOOT.  Would you mind if I put on my boots?

DUKE.  Not at all.  I think you will face the situation with more dignity if you are clothed in a seemly manner.

PROUDFOOT (*sits on sofa*).  'pon my word.  Pray go on, sir! I cannot help thinking that shrimping is an over-rated amusement.

DUKE (c.s.).  You are more likely to get your boot on if you try it on the right foot.

PROUDFOOT.  I beg your pardon.  It was an oversight.

DUKE.  Pray don't apologise.  It is a matter of indifference to me on which feet you wear your boots.

PROUDFOOT.  By the way, you don't happen to be wanting a good bootmaker, do you?

DUKE.  I do not.

PROUDFOOT.  I could have recommended you someone whose terms are reasonable and whose work is excellent.

DUKE.  Sir, I will come straight to the point.  The world we live in is small.  I regret to inform you that there is not room in it for both of us.

PROUDFOOT (*dumbfounded, foot in mid-air*).  I beg your pardon?

DUKE.  I feel sure that you are sufficiently intelligent to realise which of us is superfluous?

PROUDFOOT.  I presume you're not referring to me, sir?

DUKE (*blandly*).  Who else, my dear fellow?  Who else?

PROUDFOOT. But this is most unexpected. Why am I not wanted on this earth?

DUKE (*impressively*). Because I love the same woman as you do.

PROUDFOOT. What woman?

DUKE. Your wife.

PROUDFOOT (*stupefied*). My wife? You're not in love with my wife?

DUKE. Passionately.

PROUDFOOT (*rising, with dignity, semi-shod*). If this is a jest, sir, I consider it in doubtful taste.

DUKE. I never jest with love.

PROUDFOOT. Then, if you will pardon my frankness—you must be mad.

DUKE. Mad with the greatest passion in my life.

PROUDFOOT. Have you seen my wife?

DUKE. Fifty times.

PROUDFOOT. Perhaps you're shortsighted.

DUKE. Not at all. My sight is even abnormally keen.

PROUDFOOT. Then you must be seriously unwell. And you're positively in love with my wife?

DUKE. I have told her so with all the passion at my command.

PROUDFOOT. Then I think you show a lamentable want of decorum in repeating to me what you have said to a lady.

DUKE. Sir, let us waste no idle words. I love your wife. Is that clear to you?

PROUDFOOT. It is clear, to the verge of indelicacy.

DUKE. I have only to look at you to know it is impossible that she should love you. You're singularly plain.

PROUDFOOT. I beg to differ from you entirely. I have always been led to understand that my personal attractions are not to be despised.

DUKE. I'm sorry, but you have been grossly deceived.

PROUDFOOT. Would you have the goodness to tell me what you want?

DUKE. I want your wife.

PROUDFOOT (*thinking that he had heard wrong*). I beg your pardon.

DUKE. I love her, and I have vowed that she shall be mine.

PROUDFOOT. I have no wish to misjudge you, but I cannot help thinking this points to positive immorality.

DUKE. Are you willing to waive your rights over her in my favour?

PROUDFOOT. Certainly not. More especially since she brought me thirty thousand pounds.

DUKE. Do you think I care for filthy lucre. Keep the money, man, and give me your wife.

PROUDFOOT. But, my dear sir, these things are not done in England. It is a delusion of the Continent that we take our wives to Smithfield with a halter round their necks, and sell them to the highest bidder. We often wish we could, but we can't. Besides, I have no wish to part from my wife.

DUKE. I regret that we cannot settle the matter amicably. You insist upon the arbitrament of war.

PROUDFOOT. Do you propose to resort to violence?

DUKE (*blandly*). I propose to, in a very friendly spirit.

PROUDFOOT. That may be. But still, you are suggesting a—a duel to a man of peace.

DUKE. A duel to the death, sir.

PROUDFOOT. It is against all my principles. I have been led to believe that a duel is a very painful business—for the person who happens to be killed.

DUKE. Am I to understand that you refuse?

PROUDFOOT. I put my principles before everything.

DUKE. And this is the man whom she hesitates to sacrifice. A man who refuses to die for her.

PROUDFOOT. But it isn't for her that I refuse to die; it's entirely for myself. I have come to the seaside to rest, to eat and sleep, to take sea-baths, and, when the ladies insist upon it, to shrimp. And upon my word, I don't feel inclined to run the risk of being killed by a fire-eating foreigner. I don't even know who you are.

DUKE (*hat on and off*). I thought I told you. Don Ferdinand Francisco Maria de Lomas y Oria.

PROUDFOOT. We've never been properly introduced.

DUKE. In short, you refuse to meet me?

PROUDFOOT. In short, I do.

DUKE. I give you two minutes to think it over.

PROUDFOOT. If you give me a century, I would still refuse.

DUKE. I perceive that I must resort to extremities. (*Lightly hitting him with his glove.*) What now?

PROUDFOOT (*huffily*). I think you're very familiar. Very familiar. I hate this continental hail-fellow-well-met behaviour.

DUKE. Is it to be swords or pistols?

PROUDFOOT. It's fortunate that I have great self-command. If I hadn't, I think it is quite possible that I should strike you.

DUKE. Have the goodness to answer my question.

PROUDFOOT. I am glad that no one saw you. Glad for your sake, sir. I daresay you didn't mean to be offensive, but your vivacity was certainly liable to misconstruction.

DUKE. Did you hear what I said?

PROUDFOOT. I prefer to take no notice of it. I think you're in an excited and nervous condition. I don't know you from Adam. I don't want to know you. I think your behaviour is most irregular.

DUKE. Can a woman care for a man who cares so little for her? When your wife knows of your conduct, she will not hesitate to respond to my flame. I will go and find her.

PROUDFOOT. You may go to the devil.

(DUKE *stalks out through windows.*)

(*Moving to fireplace.*) I don't like that man at all. If he'd been an Englishman I should have thought he was—well, slapping my face.

(LADY PROUDFOOT *enters* U.S., *with her skirts pinned up, carrying shoes and stockings. Her clothes are muddy and stained with seaweed.*)

LADY PROUDFOOT (*furiously*). You're no gentleman, Sebastian You saw me slip in a puddle and you heard me call for help.

PROUDFOOT (*turning*). Don't speak to me, madam. I know all!

LADY PROUDFOOT. What do you mean, Sebastian?

PROUDFOOT. Abandoned woman, I am no longer Sebastian to you.

LADY PROUDFOOT. Oh! Oh! (*Dropping garments.*)

PROUDFOOT. This is a pretty kettle of fish, Matilda!

LADY PROUDFOOT. Explain yourself, sir!

PROUDFOOT. Silence, woman! I should have thought you would be ashamed to parade in this way parts of your body which Providence, by suggesting to the mind of man the invention of boots and stockings, has clearly indicated should be concealed.

LADY PROUDFOOT. But, darling, it is for you.

PROUDFOOT. Then you will have the goodness to reserve these exhibitions for the privacy of our bed-chamber.

LADY PROUDFOOT (*delighted*). Sebastian, I declare you're jealous.

PROUDFOOT. I'm not jealous. At least, I hoped no longer to have occasion to be so. But it appears that these foreigners are very susceptible, and therefore I command you, Matilda, to hide all that.

LADY PROUDFOOT (*coyly*). You don't mean to say that someone has been attracted by these modest charms?

PROUDFOOT. Are you surprised? So am I. *I* am dumbfounded. But the fact remains that these arts and graces of yours, these ridiculous vapours, have turned the head of an unfortunate young man.

LADY PROUDFOOT (*playfully*). Oh, Sebastian, you must be joking.

c

PROUDFOOT. I wish I were. Unfortunately, I have proofs of what I say. He had the impudence to come and tell me.

LADY PROUDFOOT (*flattered*). I really can't help it if people look at me. You ought to be pleased.

PROUDFOOT. I'm not.

LADY PROUDFOOT. Is he young?

PROUDFOOT. Don't be coy, Matilda. You know very well whom I'm talking about.

LADY PROUDFOOT. I don't, indeed. I wish I did.

PROUDFOOT. At all events, you know now that I am no longer ignorant of your disgraceful intrigue. I say no more, Matilda.

LADY PROUDFOOT. Tell me his name, Sebastian.

PROUDFOOT. He is a villain, Matilda. I refuse to discuss him. Pray go and clothe yourself decently.

LADY PROUDFOOT (*with a gasp*). Oh, Sebastian, you suspect my virtue. Ah, now I see it all. Unhappy Matilda. Oh, unjust Sebastian. How can you! How can you! (*Sobbing.*) I am innocent, Sebastian. I vow to you that I am innocent. (*Kneels at his feet and covers her eyes.*)

PROUDFOOT. I'm sure the noble Spaniard never saw her cry.

LADY PROUDFOOT. You know that I only love you. What does it matter what others think of me, so long as you have my heart.

PROUDFOOT. Matilda, will you promise never again to be flighty and flirtatious?

LADY PROUDFOOT. I'll promise anything so long as you won't doubt me.

PROUDFOOT. Then you may kiss me.

LADY PROUDFOOT (*rising and throwing herself in his arms*). You know I can never love another.

PROUDFOOT (*over her shoulder*). I wish I knew what the Spaniard sees in her!

(DUKE *appears at windows.*)

DUKE. I trust I do not intrude?

PROUDFOOT (*putting* LADY PROUDFOOT *to one side*). What the
  deuce do you want, sir?
DUKE (*recognises him*). *Caramba!* He is false! *Now* will I have
  his wife! (*Turns with a gesture of triumph and goes out.*)

QUICK CURTAIN

# ACT TWO

SCENE: *The same as Act I. Afternoon of the same day.*
*The breakfast things are cleared away and the front flap of*
*the table has been lowered: a chair has been placed before it.*
LADY PROUDFOOT *is discovered seated in the chair, plucking*
*the petals of a marguerite. The doors,* B.S., *are open.*

LADY PROUDFOOT. He loves me. He loves me not. He loves
me ... Oh, I wish I knew his name! He loves me—he loves
me not—he loves me——

(MARION *and the* COUNTESS *come in from terrace.*)

MARION. What are you doing, Lady Proudfoot?
LADY PROUDFOOT (*self-consciously rising and thrusting stalk into*
*vase*). I? I was rapt in meditation. (*Sighs.*)
COUNTESS (*smiling*). Why do you sigh so deeply? I hope
you're not suffering from an affair of the heart?
LADY PROUDFOOT (*to* MARION). Oh, my dear, don't marry
again. Men are monsters. Monsters of jealousy. (*She moves*
*dramatically to fireplace.*)
COUNTESS. What is the matter?
LADY PROUDFOOT (*tragically*). My husband knows all.
MARION (*moving* L.C.). All what?
LADY PROUDFOOT. Nothing. There's nothing to know. That's
why it's so tragic. I am an unhappy woman. Oh, if you'd
seen him. He's made such a scene.
MARION (*incredulously*). The Judge?
LADY PROUDFOOT. Oh, my dear, I shall never get over it. I've
been so unlucky as to excite an undying passion in the heart
of an unfortunate young man.
MARION. Impossible!
LADY PROUDFOOT (*turning, put out*). Not at all. It's always

happening to me. I have a fatal gift. And Sebastian's as
jealous as a tiger.

MARION. But how did the Judge hear of it?

LADY PROUDFOOT. Oh, my dear, the imprudent young man
told Sebastian himself. I swear to you that I am innocent. I
could bear it if I weren't.

COUNTESS (*moving* L.C.). But what is to be done?

LADY PROUDFOOT (*wringing her hands*). He loves me. He wor-
ships me. Sebastian knows the truth, and he has determined
to kill him.

MARION. Tell us exactly what happened.

LADY PROUDFOOT. Listen. (*Slipping into sofa.*) I came back
from shrimping, and I was dreadfully wet. I'm afraid my
dress will never look the same again.

MARION and COUNTESS (*impatiently*). Yes, yes.

LADY PROUDFOOT. Suddenly Sebastian sprang to his feet, and
faced me like a raving madman. He was as pale as death, and
his face twitched with passion. He looked at me with
clenched hands, grinding his teeth, and raucous sounds
issued from his throat.

COUNTESS. Lor! he must have looked a fright.

LADY PROUDFOOT (*rising*). "Woman!" he cried, "you have
deceived me. I have long suspected you, but now I have
proofs."

MARION. And what did you say?

LADY PROUDFOOT. I drew myself to my full height, and
answered calmly: "Sebastian, I am pure".

MARION. I wish I had seen you.

LADY PROUDFOOT (*moving* D.S.L.). At length he grew calmer,
but it is the deceitful calm that precedes the storm. Suspicion has entered like a canker in his soul, and our happiness
is for ever at an end. (*Back to* MARION C.) Oh, my dear,
protect me. Protect me from my husband. Protect me from
myself; but, above all, protect me from that audacious and
imprudent young man.

COUNTESS. And who is it?

LADY PROUDFOOT (*turning to face audience, standing between* MARION *and the* COUNTESS). It's so annoying; that's just what I don't know. He sighs at a distance, and yearns for me only from afar ... Take care, there's Sebastian. Let us dissemble.

> (*They move over* R. *to fireplace. The next three speeches are all said simultaneously and very quickly.* PROUDFOOT *watches the speakers in ominous silence as he enters through doors,* U.S.)

| | |
|---|---|
| MARION. | It's a shame to stay indoors in this beautiful weather. We really ought to go out. I'm sure it won't last much longer. |
| COUNTESS. | What a lovely gown that is. Where did you get it? You always wear such beautiful things. I envy you your dressmaker. |
| LADY PROUDFOOT. | Don't you think Sebastian's the handsomest judge on the Queen's bench? Prisoners say it's quite a pleasure to be sentenced by him. |

PROUDFOOT (*sternly, moving swiftly to* C.). Matilda!

LADY PROUDFOOT (*breaking away and throwing her arms about his neck*). Dear one, you know I am yours.

PROUDFOOT (*pushing*). I object to these public demonstrations of your affection, Matilda.

LADY PROUDFOOT (*head bowed*). You are cold, Sebastian, cold, cold.

PROUDFOOT. With the thermometer at eighty-five in the shade?

LADY PROUDFOOT (*a gesture of appeal to* MARION). You hear his brutal sarcasm?

MARION. I don't think you're nice to your wife, and you know she adores you.

LADY PROUDFOOT. If he doesn't know that now, he'll never know it.

PROUDFOOT. Silence, woman! You have lost the right to adore upon me.

LADY PROUDFOOT. Wouldn't you like to go for a walk on the sands, Sebastian?

PROUDFOOT. Do you want to meet anyone, perchance? I am unwell, Matilda. Do you understand me? I am unwell. I shall not go out again to-day.

LADY PROUDFOOT (*all devotion*). Then I will sit by your side, all the afternoon.

PROUDFOOT (*gloomily*). And to think that I came here for relaxation, and innocent amusement. How happy is the heathen Turk, who can keep his Circassian bride under lock and key. (*Moody exit.*)

LADY PROUDFOOT. There, now you've seen for yourselves. Oh, we live in parlous times. Did you hear him call me his Circassian bride? (*With great emotion.*) I shouldn't be surprised if he sewed me in a sack and threw me in the Bosphorus. (*Exultant exit.*)

COUNTESS (*sitting on sofa*). Of course the poor thing's quite, quite mad.

MARION. What on earth does it all mean?

COUNTESS. Heaven only knows. But, for someone to fall in love with Lady Proudfoot is really too strange.

MARION. Talking of adorers, I must really tell you about mine.

COUNTESS. You have so many. Do you mean my husband?

MARION. You take his passion for me very coolly. I was thinking of the noble Spaniard.

COUNTESS. Oh!

MARION. It was a horrid trick of yours to run away and leave me to his mercies.

COUNTESS. I liked his impudence in coming here. I'm sure he's bold and bad.

MARION. I couldn't get rid of the creature, and at last I was obliged to tell a little fib. I said I was married. It seemed the only way of having any peace.

COUNTESS. I suppose that drove him away?

MARION. Yes, but—he came back again, to ask for an introduction to my husband.

COUNTESS. I presume he was seized with a desire to become his bosom friend.

MARION. Not at all. He merely wanted to kill him, so that I might be free.

COUNTESS. It sounds eminently reasonable. I like your Spaniard, for he's very bold and bad.

MARION. I only got rid of him by pretending I was going to throw myself out of the window.

COUNTESS. If he'd only had the sense to look, he'd have known that you couldn't possibly hurt yourself. And is he as good looking as he seems from a distance?

MARION. Better, if anything.

COUNTESS. I wonder if he really loves you?

MARION (*bridling*). Of course he loves me. There's not the slightest shadow of a doubt of that.

COUNTESS. And yet you have the heart to break his?

MARION (*with a shrug*). A broken heart never prevents a man from eating a hearty dinner.

COUNTESS. I really believe my husband's your most dangerous admirer, after all.

MARION. My dear, what nonsense!

COUNTESS. I promise you I don't care. When I married a Frenchman I made up my mind that I would never be jealous. He's the most flirtatious person in the world, but if any of the ladies to whom he says pretty things took him at his word, no one would be more scandalised than himself.

(*Enter* CHALFORD *through windows*, L.)

MARION. Ah, here is the Captain.

CHALFORD (*presenting himself, and then*). What news, dear lady? How is my Lucy?

COUNTESS. Is Lucy ill?

CHALFORD (*tragically*). Don't attempt to spare my feelings. Let me know the worst at once.

MARION. Don't be so silly. There's nothing the matter with her. It was a mere scratch.

(LUCY *enters through doors, be-shawled.*)

There, you can see for yourself. (*Slips into armchair,* D.S.R.)

LUCY. I didn't know anyone was here.

CHALFORD. I came to ask after your precious health.

LUCY (*joining him* C.S.). I am quite well, thank you.

CHALFORD (*stepping back*). For my sake, Lucy, you must be careful; you're sure it won't show?

LUCY. Quite sure.

CHALFORD (*up to her again*). And even if it did, you know that I would never love you less.

LUCY. Now give me my tapestry. I mean to work in the garden, and you, sir, may sit by my side and hold my wool.

CHALFORD. Sweet charmer. (*Takes up tapestry from table by sofa.*)

LUCY. Oh, Marion, I've just seen the noble Spaniard wandering round and round the house.

CHALFORD (*stopping*). What Spaniard?

LUCY. Nobody you know, Mr. Inquisitive.

COUNTESS. Captain C. thinks he has the right to be inquisitive.

MARION. Now, Lucy, don't be such a tease.

LUCY (*with a curtsey*). It's a noble Spaniard that I see on my walks abroad.

MARION. You're not obliged to look at the people that you pass in the street.

CHALFORD (*fuming*). It is fortunate that I'm not of a jealous temper.

LUCY. I really can't help seeing him if the man's there every time I look out of the window.

COUNTESS. You're not obliged to look out of your window.

MARION. The eye of well-brought up young ladies should be under the strictest control.

LUCY. Prunes and prisms.

COUNTESS. Hoity-toity!

CHALFORD. I must say that I should like some kind of explanation.

MARION. My dear friend, it's only Lucy's nonsense. Don't you see that she's quizzing you?

LUCY. You look such a fright when you're rather cross.

CHALFORD. I can't help my personal appearance, Lucy. The Begum of Monsore had no fault to find with it.

MARION. Don't be so foolish. You're wasting time which you might employ much more profitably in saying pleasant things to one another.

CHALFORD. Yes; that's very true.

LUCY. You jealous wretch! Come into the garden!

CHALFORD. Do you love me still?

LUCY. I shan't tell you.

(*Goes out. As* CHALFORD *is following her,* MARY JANE *comes in through doors.*)

MARY. The Spanish gentleman is here again, mum.

CHALFORD (*stopping and turning*). What!

LUCY (*appearing again*). Aren't you coming, Adolphus?

CHALFORD. Yes, my dear . . . The Spaniard! I wonder why?

LUCY (*laughing*). You jealous creature.

(CHALFORD *follows* LUCY *out.*)

COUNTESS. It was hardly worth while to tell the man you were married.

MARION (*rising*). Say that I'm engaged.

MARY. Very well, mum.

COUNTESS. No, no—do see him!

MARION. Nothing will induce me to.

COUNTESS. Please. I want so much to know what he's like when you see him quite close.

MARION. He only wants to make love to me.

COUNTESS. Oh, my dear, let him. When you're fifty no one will want to.

(*As* MARY JANE *reaches the doors the* DUKE *enters. Exit* MARY JANE, *closing doors.*)

DUKE. I'm afraid you are engaged.

MARION (*to the* COUNTESS). Madame la Comtesse de Moret. The Duke of Hermanos.

DUKE (*bowing*). Marquis of Alcala, Count of Triana.

MARION (*quickly*). Of course, I forgot. A grandee of Spain, with the right to wear his hat in the presence of the King. But the King doesn't happen to be here . . .

DUKE. No more does my hat.

MARION. And what can I do for you?

DUKE. I have a thousand things to say to you, all of the most import——

COUNTESS (*rising*). I will leave you. (*To* DUKE, *bowing*.) Sir. (*Exit through windows.*)

MARION. May I ask you to say once and for all what you have to say. This is the third time to-day that you have obliged me to listen to you. I hope it will be the last.

DUKE. Not at all.

MARION. You're exhausting my patience.

DUKE. I have something new to tell you.

MARION. The time I have at your disposal is excessively limited.

DUKE. I have seen your husband.

MARION (*dumbfounded*). What!

DUKE. I have seen your husband.

MARION. Whom?

DUKE. Mr. Nairne. I have spoken to him. And since we could not come to an understanding, I slapped his face.

MARION. Impossible.

DUKE. I used no unnecessary violence. But that is not all.

MARION (*trying to restrain her laughter*). Is there more to come?

DUKE. I have a matter the most delicate to impart to you.

MARION. Fancy!

DUKE. I wish I could spare you. But my life's happiness depends upon it. Your husband is unworthy of you. He loves another.

MARION. You don't say so!

DUKE. Poor creature! And you thought he loved you. Poor, poor Marion. I have robbed you of your dear illusions, but it was needful. I have killed the love in your heart, but another love will take its place—love for me.

MARION. I have not the least doubt now that you ought to be shut up in a madhouse.

DUKE. It wouldn't be strange if the flower you gave me had bereft me of my senses, or if the touch of your rosy fingers had driven my poor wits crazy.

MARION. I beg you to remember that you took the flower by main force, and you only kissed my hand because I was in a state of considerable agitation.

DUKE. Marion. (*Kisses her.*)

MARION (*starts, smiles, and gives him a roguish glance—gasping*). It's monstrous that you should take such liberties with—a married woman.

DUKE. Have you never dreamed of a castle in Spain? I can give you a castle where kings in armour and infantas in cloth of gold have held their revels. Eagles soar above its towers, and snow-capped mountains guard it round and round.

MARION. My castle in Spain has a river near it, and a shady wood.

DUKE. A babbling brook runs at the base of mine, and the wind of summer sighs delicious things in a wood of chestnut trees.

MARION. You might hate me after a week.

DUKE. I have jewels that have decked queens of Castile, and you shall wear them. I have great stores of silks from Eastern looms that have lain in my treasury for a hundred years.

MARION. I wonder why you love me?

DUKE. Marion! (*Puts his arm about her waist.*)

MARION. You certainly make love very attractively.

DUKE. To-night as soon as it grows dark, I will await you behind the villa with post-horses. We will fly together.

MARION. You forget my husband.

DUKE. Can you think of him after what I have told you?

MARION (*dramatically*). You have told me nothing that I did
not know before.

DUKE. You knew that your husband loved another?

MARION. Alas, sir, we are not masters of our affections.

DUKE. But I struck him, and he would not accept my challenge.

MARION. I love him.

DUKE. It is impossible. It is I you love, I who am willing to
fight the whole world to gain you—to slap the face of every
man in Europe. At present, you are suffering from the blow
which I have administered. When you are alone, I feel sure
that you will recover your equilibrium. I shall go now to
order the post-horses and then I will return.

MARION. It is quite useless. I am resolved.

DUKE. Do you prefer to come with me?

MARION. No.

DUKE. Of course you're right, you're always right. You
naturally cannot leave the house in my company. Very
well, I shall be behind the villa at eight o'clock to-night.

MARION. Don't be absurd.

DUKE (*very quickly, allowing her no opportunity to interrupt*). Is
the time inconvenient? Say nine, then, or ten, eleven, twelve,
one, two, three, any hour you like. In any case, you have
only to send me word . . . but not by letter. We must
take no risks. Ah, I have him. The simplest ways are
always best. I will send you a bouquet, and when you are
ready, throw it out of the window. I shall be waiting and I
will fly to you. Do you understand? Fling it out of the
window and I will fling myself at your feet.

MARION (*bursting out at last*). For goodness' sake, listen to me.

DUKE. What is the use of words, when our hearts understand one another? My angel, farewell. I will send the flowers at once. Marion—Marion! (*He catches her in his arms and kisses her then—goes out, flinging wide the doors,* U.S.)

MARION. How dare you! How dare you! How dare you!

(COUNTESS *returns through windows.*)

COUNTESS. Has he quite gone?

MARION. It was hateful of you to make me see him. You don't know what nonsense he's been talking.

COUNTESS (*coming to* C.). Really.

MARION. He wants me to elope with him, and he's going to keep post-horses outside the house all night.

COUNTESS. It will be the best proof of his affection.

MARION. Why?

COUNTESS. Because it'll be very expensive. You can always measure a man's love best by the money he's willing to waste on you.

MARION. And do you know, he had the impudence to *try* and kiss me. But, of course, I showed him at once that I was not the sort of woman to put up with a liberty.

COUNTESS. What did you do?

MARION. I froze him with a glance.

COUNTESS (*with a chuckle*). You know, I was just outside and I couldn't help hearing everything that passed.

MARION. Kate!

COUNTESS. And unless I am very much mistaken you didn't freeze him very effectively.

MARION. I'm sure I don't know what you mean!

COUNTESS. Merely that he kissed you, not only once but twice, and as far as I could judge, you kept your indignation well under control.

MARION. You don't mean to say you suspect me of allowing myself to be kissed by a total stranger?

COUNTESS. My dear child, do be reasonable. You weren't happy with your first husband because he didn't care for you. Try again with this man who adores you.

MARION. But I can't bear the sight of him!

COUNTESS. I don't know so much about that.

MARION (*pulling the bell-cord* R.). Well, I'll prove it.

COUNTESS. How?

MARION. I shall ask the Judge to come to me. He's the only man in the house, the only man I can go to.

MARY (*as she enters*). Yes, ma'am?

MARION. Ask Sir Sebastian to come to me.

MARY. Very well, mum. (*Exit.*)

MARION (*going to* COUNTESS, C.). The thing has gone beyond a joke, and I mean to put an end to it. I propose to get rid of the noble Spaniard once for all.

COUNTESS. The best way to do that is to marry him.

MARION. He didn't kiss me, Kate.

COUNTESS (*moving away a little to* L.). Well, we'll each keep our own opinion on the matter.

(*Enter* PROUDFOOT.)

PROUDFOOT. Did you send for me, dear Marion?

MARION (*moving to him,* C.). I want you to do me a great service.

PROUDFOOT. My dear child, you know that I am at your command for anything and everything.

MARION. I knew that I could depend on you.

PROUDFOOT. Well, what is it?

MARION. Next time a Spaniard comes here, calling himself the Duke of Hermanos, I shall be obliged if you will kick him downstairs.

PROUDFOOT. What! ! !

MARION. Or if you prefer it, you may throw him out of the window.

PROUDFOOT. But, my dear Marion . . .

MARION (*to the* COUNTESS *as she passes over to windows*, L.). There. (*Goes out by window, followed by* COUNTESS.)

PROUDFOOT (*moving to fireplace*). Kick him downstairs! Matilda! Matilda!

(LADY PROUDFOOT *enters*, U.S.)

LADY PROUDFOOT. Did you call me?

PROUDFOOT. Woman, put on your bonnet.

LADY PROUDFOOT. Are we going out?

PROUDFOOT. Should I ask you to put on your bonnet to remain indoors?

LADY PROUDFOOT. Where are we going?

PROUDFOOT. Woman, put on your bonnet.

LADY PROUDFOOT. Shall I take my shawl?

PROUDFOOT. Damn your shawl, madam!

LADY PROUDFOOT. What do you mean, Sebastian? Where are you going to take me? . . . The Bosphorus! ! (*With alarm.*)

PROUDFOOT. What the devil are you talking about, Matilda?

LADY PROUDFOOT. Sebastian!

PROUDFOOT. Where's my hat?

LADY PROUDFOOT. Oh, you still suspect me?

PROUDFOOT. Where's my hat?

LADY PROUDFOOT. But I am pure, Sebastian. Pure as the newborn lamb.

PROUDFOOT. Where's my hat?

LADY PROUDFOOT. I've had my temptations, but I've never yielded. Not once have other lips than yours touched even my brow.

PROUDFOOT (*going out*). Where's my hat? (*Exit through doors* U.S., *turning* R. *as he goes off.*)

LADY PROUDFOOT. I wish I knew his name!

(MARY JANE *appears through doors* U.S., *from* L., *with a bouquet of flowers.*)

MARY. My lady.

LADY PROUDFOOT. Oh! Are they for me?

MARY. A gentleman brought them, and told me to give them to my mistress.

LADY PROUDFOOT (*much agitated*). Oh, leave me. Leave me!
> (MARY JANE *goes out,* LADY PROUDFOOT *moves to fire-place* R.)

I wonder if there's a letter. He must be as beautiful as his flowers. ,
> (PROUDFOOT *comes in with hat.*)

PROUDFOOT. Now, Matilda.

LADY PROUDFOOT (*hiding the bouquet in front of her*). Great heavens! (*Hiding it behind her.*)

PROUDFOOT. What is the matter with you, Matilda?

LADY PROUDFOOT. Nothing.

PROUDFOOT. Why are you scratching your back?

LADY PROUDFOOT. I wouldn't do anything so vulgar, Sebastian.

PROUDFOOT. Turn round, madam.

LADY PROUDFOOT (*trembling like a leaf*). Sebastian!

PROUDFOOT (*swinging her round*). A nosegay! (*Takes the flowers.*)

LADY PROUDFOOT (*falling on her knees, and joining her hands*). I am innocent, Sebastian.

PROUDFOOT. This is too much. I leave you for one moment to fetch my hat, and when I return I find you with a nosegay.

LADY PROUDFOOT (*clutching* PROUDFOOT's *knees*). Don't judge me hastily. I can explain all.

PROUDFOOT. Rise to your feet, abandoned woman. Whence are these wages of sin?

LADY PROUDFOOT (*rising, using* PROUDFOOT *as a staff*). I don't know.

PROUDFOOT. You don't know? You're not a conjurer.

LADY PROUDFOOT (*helplessly*). No, I'm not a conjurer.

PROUDFOOT. They can't have grown suddenly in the hollow of your hand! Here is my hat—produce a white rabbit from it, or a pot of geraniums.

D

LADY PROUDFOOT. I *know* appearances are against me, but I am innocent.

PROUDFOOT. Whence came these flowers?

LADY PROUDFOOT. They've just this moment been sent me. But I swear to you, on the memory of my sainted mother, that I don't know who they're from. (*She tries a little weeping.*)

PROUDFOOT. You forget that I am a judge and am accustomed to deal with criminals. Guilt is stamped on your face.

LADY PROUDFOOT. Oh, that I should live to see this day!

PROUDFOOT. Someone came to this room while I was fetching my hat?

LADY PROUDFOOT (*weakly, sinking into sofa*). I—I forget.

PROUDFOOT. Your agitation betrays you. Men have been hanged, Matilda, on less evidence than this.

LADY PROUDFOOT. Oh, I wish I'd taken the advice of my Aunt Sarah, who went down on her bended knees to me and begged me not to marry a common lawyer.

PROUDFOOT. Do not attempt to throw me off the scent with irrelevant observations. You have to deal with a master of cross examination.

LADY PROUDFOOT. How can you talk to me like that when it was my own father who gave you your first brief. And I could have had my cousin, Colonel Kindersley of the 52nd.

PROUDFOOT. Enough, woman! This is how I treat the presents of your lover. (*Strides to stage L. and throws bouquet out of window.*)

LADY PROUDFOOT (*wringing her hands*). You will bitterly regret this when I am no more.

PROUDFOOT (*moving back to C.*). Ha!

(DUKE *appears at the windows with the flowers in his hand.*)

DUKE. May I inquire who threw these flowers out of the window?

PROUDFOOT. I did.

DUKE. Do you want me to kill you?

PROUDFOOT. I will not let you send flowers to my wife.

LADY PROUDFOOT (*into the crook of her arm*). It is he!

DUKE. I will send your wife as many flowers as I choose. (*Dumps bouquet in a vase on table, L.*) Look. And if you dare to touch them, beware. I say nothing but—beware. (*Stalks out by window, threateningly.*)

LADY PROUDFOOT (*under the other arm*). What a thorough nobleman!

PROUDFOOT (*boiling*). I will have that man's blood. I am a man of peace, but there are limits to my endurance. I will prove to you, Matilda, that your cousin, Colonel Kindersley of the 52nd., had not more spirit than I. Give me his blood, I say. Give me his blood!

LADY PROUDFOOT (*with outstretched arms*). My darling, what would you do with it?

PROUDFOOT. I will wallow in it, Matilda.

LADY PROUDFOOT. Oh, this is romance.

PROUDFOOT (*gesticulating*). Blood! Blood!

LADY PROUDFOOT (*rising, with a move to fireplace*). Do you wish to kill him because he loves me?

PROUDFOOT. Blood! Blood!

LADY PROUDFOOT (*turning*). He cannot help it. After all, it is not so strange.

PROUDFOOT. How dare you defend him to my face? Shame, I say, shame! Come, give me his blood.

(LADY PROUDFOOT *goes towards the window.*)

Not that way, Matilda. You might meet the Spaniard.

LADY PROUDFOOT (*stopping in her tracks, L.C.*). A Spaniard! Oh, Byron, Byron. Don Juan's parents lived beside the river. A noble stream and called the Guadalquiver.

PROUDFOOT. Look at me, Matilda. Now side face. (*After a pause.*) I cannot understand how she has inspired him with this mad passion.

LADY PROUDFOOT. Why so thoughtful, my Sebastian?

PROUDFOOT. Follow me, Jezebel.

(PROUDFOOT *goes out by doors* U.S. LADY PROUDFOOT
*picks up flowers and smells them lovingly.* LUCY *enters from
windows,* L.)

LUCY. Oh, what lovely flowers!

PROUDFOOT (*off*). Jezebel.

(LADY PROUDFOOT *thrusts flowers at* LUCY, *having lost
her presence of mind.*)

LUCY (*surprised*). Are they for me?

LADY PROUDFOOT. Take great care of them.

LUCY. Dear, dear Adolphus.

(PROUDFOOT, *appearing in doorway.*)

PROUDFOOT. Woman!! (*Disappears again.*)

LADY PROUDFOOT. "Sun burnt his cheek, his forehead high and
pale;
The sable curls in wild profusion veil."

(PROUDFOOT, *re-entering.*)

PROUDFOOT. *Jezebel,* put on your bonnet! (*Exit.*)

LADY PROUDFOOT. I'm coming—I'm coming. (*Moves to doors,*
U.S., *turns.*) Lucy, before I go. I must tell you one thing. If
I'm found at the bottom of the Bosphorus, I shall not have
gone there of my own accord. (*Exit.*)

LUCY. Lady Proudfoot!

LADY PROUDFOOT (*returning*). Farewell, I say no more, farewell.
(*Exit.*)

(LUCY *takes one or two of the flowers and puts them in her
dress.* CHALFORD *enters* U.S. *She turns round and sees him.*)

CHALFORD. By Jupiter, those are damned fine roses.

LUCY. Beautiful.

CHALFORD. And, may I ask, who sent them to you?

LUCY. I haven't an idea.

CHALFORD. How is that?

LUCY. Not the vaguest, faintest, smallest shadow of an idea.

CHALFORD. My dear Lucy I beg you to tell me.

LUCY (*teasing*). A gentleman sent them to me.

CHALFORD. An old gentleman?

LUCY. A young gentleman, who's rather handsome and who loves me.

CHALFORD. Not as much as I do, I presume?

LUCY. Every bit.

CHALFORD. And may I venture to inquire his name?

LUCY. I think you know it, foolish creature.

CHALFORD. If I ask you, it is evidently because I don't. I insist on knowing who sent you these flowers?

LUCY (*seriously*). Didn't you?

CHALFORD. You must know I didn't.

LUCY. Then I haven't a notion.

CHALFORD. Yet you accept them and you put them in your dress. And when I come in you tell me that *I* sent them. Come, come, Lucy. I beg you not to jest. Please tell me the plain truth. I have the right to know it.

LUCY. Indeed?

CHALFORD. Am I not your affianced husband?

LUCY. We're not married *yet*, and the tone in which you speak gives me the right to refuse to answer.

CHALFORD. That's a very clever way of avoiding a difficult explanation.

LUCY. And pray what do you mean by that, Captain Chalford?

CHALFORD. Nothing at all, Miss Lucy, I assure you.

LUCY. I thought you sent me the flowers, and I told you so frankly.

CHALFORD. You told me that because I surprised you smelling them.

LUCY. Would you kindly explain yourself, sir?

CHALFORD. I have nothing to explain, ma'am.

LUCY. I understand, all the same. And if you no longer care for me, it would be better to tell me so frankly instead of picking a frivolous quarrel.

CHALFORD. And you, ma'am, if you really loved me would say frankly who sent you those wretched flowers.

LUCY. But I tell you I don't know, and to show you how little I care for them . . . (*Moves swiftly to window and flings them out.*) There!

CHALFORD. Lucy!

LUCY. I will never forgive you. Adieu for ever.

CHALFORD. Lucy!

(LUCY *goes out* U.S. *quickly*, CHALFORD *following her, as the* DUKE, *flowers in hand, appears at the window* L.)

DUKE. This time there can be no mistake.

CHALFORD (*arrested at door*). What the devil do you want?

DUKE. I don't know that it's any business of yours, but, in point of fact, I want the answer to my bouquet.

CHALFORD. Then it was you who sent it?

DUKE. It was.

CHALFORD. And why, sir, if you please?

DUKE. Among other things, as a proof of my unbounded passion.

CHALFORD (*coming down* C. *to join* DUKE). You have the most confounded audacity.

DUKE. It's a family characteristic.

CHALFORD. You're not by any chance under the impression that your unbounded passion is returned?

DUKE. This bouquet is a sign of it.

CHALFORD. Do you mean to say it was a declaration of love?

DUKE. More. It was a signal.

CHALFORD. Perfidious creature.

DUKE. You were there when she threw it?

CHALFORD. I was indeed, sir.

DUKE. Then there really is no mistake. I will order the post-horses at once.

CHALFORD (*stopping him*). Stay, sir.

DUKE. And why, if you please?

CHALFORD. Because we both love the same lady. But it is I she cares for—not you.

DUKE. You are mistaken, my friend.

CHALFORD. She has vowed a hundred times that she loves me.

DUKE. Her sentiments have changed. For three weeks I have dogged her footsteps night and day. Such constancy could not fail to touch her.

CHALFORD. She must have found your conduct infinitely tedious.

DUKE. In all cases, if you dispute my right, I am willing to give you satisfaction.

CHALFORD. I'm delighted to hear it. A duel will give me an appetite for supper.

DUKE. The more I kill, the greater will be her regard for me.

CHALFORD. Captain Chalford of the Heavy Dragoons, at your service.

DUKE. I am the Duke of Hermanos. One favour only I beg of you, and that is that we settle the matter quickly. I am much pressed for time.

CHALFORD. Nothing could suit me better. I will meet you on the sands outside the town in two hours from now.

DUKE. Sir, your very humble servant.

CHALFORD. And now I leave this house never to return. Perfidious creature. (*Exit through windows.*)

DUKE. Curse me five times, a rival. Don Whiskerandos.

(MARION *comes in door,* U.S.)

MARION. Have you taken up your abode in this house, sir?

DUKE (*proffering her the bouquet, kneeling*). You threw the flowers from the window, and I have come.

MARION (*declining the bouquet*). I?

DUKE. I have something new to tell you.

MARION. Pray keep it to yourself, then. I'm quite tired of your absurdities.

DUKE. In two hours the man you love will be dead.

MARION. What are you talking about, now?

DUKE. I know, now, why you scorned my flame. Not because you loved your husband, but because you loved another.

MARION (*ironically*). And I suppose you've seen him, too?

DUKE (*rises*). I hope to cross swords with him in two hours.

MARION (*dumbfounded*). You're going to fight a duel with the man I love? And who the—the—the—deuce is he?

DUKE. Don Whiskerandos.

MARION. I haven't the pleasure of his acquaintance.

DUKE. Captain Chalford of the Heavy Dragoons.

MARION. Captain Chalford?

DUKE. Yes, madam.

MARION. Do you mean to say the Captain is in love with me?

DUKE. He loves you madly. He loves you to distraction.

MARION. How do you know?

DUKE. He told me so. But no matter, in two hours he will be as dead as mutton. I will send you his whiskers on a charger. (*Sweeps out windows, L., flinging bouquet back on to the table, poetically.*)

CURTAIN

# ACT THREE

SCENE: *Same as Act II. Late evening of the same day.*

*The lamps are lit and the bouquet is in a vase on the table.*
LUCY *is alone by the open window,* L., *book in hand. The doors,* B.S., *open and* MARY JANE *enters, followed by the* COUNTESS.

MARY. The Countess de Moret. (*Exit, leaving doors open.*)
COUNTESS (*at door*). Well?

(LUCY *gives a deep sigh.*)

(*Sweeping to* C.) Oh, my dear, what a sigh.
LUCY. I shall never do anything but sigh now.
COUNTESS (*sitting on sofa*). How dreadful. And they say it's so fattening.
LUCY. I don't care if I do grow fat; my life is quite finished.
COUNTESS. Is that why you have put on your new gown?
LUCY. I couldn't go to the ball in rags.
COUNTESS. Oh! You're going to the ball to-night?
LUCY. Only to show Adolphus I don't care.
COUNTESS. I see.
LUCY. I've made up my mind that I will never marry.
COUNTESS (*with mock seriousness*). I think you're very wise. Marriage is such a risk.
LUCY (*holding out her book*). You see, I've begun to improve my mind already.
COUNTESS. What are you reading?
LUCY. Mr. Tupper's poems. They're so beautiful. I think I shall learn them by heart.
COUNTESS. I've sent for the Captain.
LUCY (*with a little cry*). Oh!

COUNTESS. I'm quite sure there's some mistake. I believe he's just as much in love with you as ever.

LUCY (*with dignity, moving forward and putting book on table*). I don't wish to hear his name mentioned. He's a villain and a deceiver.

COUNTESS. I hope he'll be here in ten minutes, and we'll ask him for an explanation.

LUCY. Here?

(PROUDFOOT *and* LADY PROUDFOOT—*the latter pale and dishevelled, and supported by* MARY JANE—*enter from* U.S.)

COUNTESS (*rising*). Good gracious!

PROUDFOOT. I feel very unwell.

LADY PROUDFOOT. Why doesn't that floor keep still, Sebastian?

LUCY. What is the matter?

LADY PROUDFOOT (*moving to the* COUNTESS, R.). We went on the sea, like Lord Byron.

PROUDFOOT. I hate these poets.

COUNTESS (*to* MARY JANE). Do fetch some cognac.

(*Exit* MARY JANE.)

LADY PROUDFOOT (*sitting on sofa*). We went on the sea. It looked so romantic—from the beach. And the boat went up like this and down like that.

PROUDFOOT. *Don't move*, Jezebel!

LADY PROUDFOOT. I wish I *were* at the bottom of the Bosphorus.

COUNTESS. I only married a Frenchman because I'm such a bad sailor. When my husband proposed to me I accepted, rather than cross the Channel again.

PROUDFOOT (*moving to sit at chair below table*, L.). And yet there are people who extol a life on the ocean wave.

COUNTESS. I notice that they generally take good care to remain on dry land.

(*Enter* MARY JANE.)

MARY (*bringing the brandy*). Here it is, mum.

LADY PROUDFOOT. Thank you. (PROUDFOOT *drinks brandy*.) I think I'm going to die, Sebastian. Oh, Byron, you have much to answer for.

(MARY JANE *takes glass and goes out*.)

PROUDFOOT. If the noble Spaniard only saw her now.

LUCY. Oh, Lady Proudfoot, why don't you read Mr. Tupper instead. He's so much more genteel.

LADY PROUDFOOT (*suddenly*). Assist me. (*Smart exit, supported by* LUCY.)

PROUDFOOT. I'm beginning to feel very much better. The recollection of Matilda in the throes of *mal de mer* acts as a positive tonic.

COUNTESS. You'll eat a capital supper, I'll be bound.

PROUDFOOT. I hope that I shall do justice to any meal that a bountiful Providence places before me. But is the Count, your husband, not going to join us?

COUNTESS. The wretch hasn't come home yet. I can't make out what has become of him.

(MARY JANE *re-enters*.)

MARY (*to* PROUDFOOT). The Spanish gentleman presents his compliments, and would like a few words with you, sir.

COUNTESS. What can he want? (*Rising*.) I'll leave you, shall I?

PROUDFOOT (*rising*). I would much sooner see him in the presence of witnesses.

COUNTESS. Oh no, I'm sure he wants to see you alone. (*Exit* L.)

PROUDFOOT. Tell the Duke that I'm busy—and that—and that I'm not at all well.

(*The* DUKE *comes in*, U.S., *with foils and a case of pistols*.)

DUKE. How fortunate. (*To* MARY JANE.) You may go.

MARY. Yes, sir. (*Exit, closing doors*.)

DUKE (*cordially, moving forward*). The very man I wanted to see.

PROUDFOOT. I'm sure the pleasure is mutual. (*Pointing to the arms*.) I see you've been making some purchases.

DUKE. I have. (*Puts "purchases" on table.*)

PROUDFOOT (*nervously*). And may I ask what you propose to do with these charming toys?

DUKE. I propose to kill your wife's lover.

PROUDFOOT (*flabbergasted*). I beg your pardon? D'you mean to tell me that my wife has a lover?

DUKE. I do.

PROUDFOOT. How do you know?

DUKE. I have seen him.

PROUDFOOT (*dumbfounded*). I don't understand . . . Then it is not you who love my wife?

DUKE. It is. There are two of us. There may be more, for all I know.

PROUDFOOT. Impossible. There can't be another.

DUKE. It will be wise when you do not contradict me. I tell you there are at least two of us.

PROUDFOOT. What *will* they say in Bedford Square?

DUKE. We have just had a talk about it.

PROUDFOOT. You and my wife?

DUKE. I and her lover. We are to meet in an hour from now on the beach outside the town.

PROUDFOOT. I shall be delighted to hear that you have inflicted serious injury on the gentleman in question.

DUKE. Have no fear. In an hour he will be no more or less.

PROUDFOOT. My dear Duke, I shall be eternally grateful to you.

DUKE. How so?

PROUDFOOT. In ridding yourself of a rival, it must be plain that you rid me of one also.

DUKE (*with extreme politeness*). You will forgive me if I remind you that there is no room in this world for you.

PROUDFOOT. For me?

DUKE. It must be plain. First the lover, then the husband. I come to tell you the good news.

PROUDFOOT. I am full of gratitude for your consideration.

DUKE. Not at all. But you may take it as a mark of my high esteem that I give you the second place.

PROUDFOOT. I confess that I fail to gather your meaning.

DUKE (*getting foil from table*). It is some time since I fought a duel. I shall require a moment to get my hand in. I will despatch you in very quick march.

PROUDFOOT. At first glance I see no reason for self-congratulation in that.

DUKE. Of course, if you wish me to take you first . . .

PROUDFOOT. I wouldn't disturb your arrangements for a moment.

DUKE. Why should we waste the priceless minutes? No time is like the present.

PROUDFOOT. I promise you that I'm in no hurry. I should look upon it as a matter for eternal regret if our acquaintance were cut off after so brief a time.

DUKE (*lunging*). My wrist is as supple as ever it was. Take the foil, my dear fellow. I trust I shall find you an antagonist worthy of my skill. (*Offers foil to* PROUDFOOT, *who takes it tremblingly.*)

PROUDFOOT (*aside*). I have only one hope; Matilda.

DUKE. By the way, have you made your will?

PROUDFOOT. Good gracious! It had slipped my memory. Could you spare me for two minutes?

DUKE. With pleasure, my dear sir, with pleasure. You need have no fear about the future of your widow. She will be handsomely provided for.

PROUDFOOT. I have a nephew in straitened circumstances.

DUKE. Leave him all you have.

PROUDFOOT. It's too kind of you. Pray take a seat.

DUKE. I'm glad you have made up your mind to take the first place.

PROUDFOOT. It's too good of you to give me the chance.

DUKE. My dear fellow, I would never cease to reproach myself if I did not treat my wife's first husband with all possible respect.

PROUDFOOT. The delicacy of your sentiments fills me with admiration. (*Exit* U.S.)

DUKE (*benignly*). Charming fellow. Husband and lover. I will slit them like capons, and then surely she cannot doubt my love.

(LADY PROUDFOOT *comes in, dramatically alarmed, a shawl about her. The ensuing scene is played with many asides.*)

LADY PROUDFOOT. Mercy, noble stranger, mercy.

DUKE. Who the devil is this?

LADY PROUDFOOT. I know all. All! I know that you want to kill him.

DUKE (*aside*). It must be the young man's mother. (*After a pause.*) Compose yourself, madam, I beg you to compose yourself.

LADY PROUDFOOT. Swear to me that you will not fight this duel.

DUKE. Alas! I fear events already come too near.

LADY PROUDFOOT. No, no, it cannot be. I know you're good. It is thus I dreamed of you, handsome as Don Juan and desperate as Lara. Don't rob me of my illusions. What else have we poor females to live for but our illusions and our love?

DUKE. Always the aged mother's despair is an affecting sight! You know my love and yet you bid me pause?

LADY PROUDFOOT. Ah, but it is in the name of that love which, all unknowing, I have aroused in your bosom . . .

DUKE (*dumbfounded*). I beg your pardon?

LADY PROUDFOOT. In the name of that sacred love I beg you to forbear. And, believe me, I will not be ungrateful.

DUKE. I'm afraid I do not quite understand.

LADY PROUDFOOT. Must I explain more clearly. You might have spared me that. I can never forget my duty to my husband, but I will be a sister to you.

DUKE. Madam, even that does not daunt me.

LADY PROUDFOOT.  If one pure kiss upon your brow could assuage these evil passions, one chaste embrace . . .

DUKE.  Poor, poor creature. Her son's danger has deranged her mind.

LADY PROUDFOOT.  And don't forget that you alone are the cause of all this trouble.

DUKE.  How so, dear lady?

LADY PROUDFOOT.  I'll not blame you, because you are a Spaniard and unacquainted with English ways; but, really, really you shouldn't have declared your mad passion to my husband.

DUKE.  Who?

LADY PROUDFOOT.  We manage these things better in England. The husband is always the last person to know the truth.

DUKE.  You continue to speak of your husband. But I have not the acquaintance of him.

LADY PROUDFOOT.  Yet you wish to kill him.

DUKE.  Not at all! It is your son.

LADY PROUDFOOT.  But, to the best of my belief, I haven't got a son.

DUKE.  Is not my rival your son?

LADY PROUDFOOT.  Your rival?

DUKE.  The paramour of her I love?

LADY PROUDFOOT (*with much dignity*).  Know, sir, that Matilda Proudfoot has never had a paramour.

DUKE.  I must confess that I am indifferent to the intrigues of the Broadfoot!

LADY PROUDFOOT.  And yet you say you love me?

DUKE.  Never on my life.

LADY PROUDFOOT.  You told my husband so.

DUKE (*thunderstruck*).  I?

LADY PROUDFOOT.  He was here when you committed that mad act of sending me a nosegay.

DUKE.  What wild imaginations could think those flowers were for you?

LADY PROUDFOOT. Did you send them to the object of your affections?

DUKE. I did.

LADY PROUDFOOT. I am that unhappy object.

DUKE. You? You!

LADY PROUDFOOT (*drawing herself up*). My lord!

DUKE. What can have put such a fantastic idea into your head?

LADY PROUDFOOT. What is there fantastic about it?

DUKE. Madam, the age of miracles is past.

LADY PROUDFOOT. I don't know what you mean, sir.

DUKE. It is Mrs. Nairne I am enamoured of.

LADY PROUDFOOT. Marion? Oh! Then why did you challenge Sebastian?

DUKE. And who the devil is he?

LADY PROUDFOOT. The handsome military-looking man with whom you were just now.

DUKE. Is he not her husband?

LADY PROUDFOOT. Certainly not, he is mine.

DUKE. Then keep him, madam; in any case I have found my Marion's lover. When I have done with him, I'll seek her husband—— (*Takes up his arms and stalks out L.*)

LADY PROUDFOOT (*tragically—moving to fireplace, R.*). Impostor! Impostor!

(PROUDFOOT, *coming in timidly.*)

PROUDFOOT. Have you calmed him?

LADY PROUDFOOT. Sebastian, prepare yourself for single combat!

PROUDFOOT. With the Spaniard?

LADY PROUDFOOT. Sebastian, I shall never survive this day.

PROUDFOOT. Matilda!

LADY PROUDFOOT. He has outraged me—— (*Sinks into sofa.*)

PROUDFOOT. Matilda!

LADY PROUDFOOT. In—my tenderest susceptibilities.

PROUDFOOT. What *do* you mean?

LADY PROUDFOOT. The worst, the very worst. Matilda Proudfoot is undone.

PROUDFOOT. Serpent!

LADY PROUDFOOT. It's Marion he's in love with.

PROUDFOOT (*with a great sigh of relief*). Marion! Now I understand everything. He didn't know Marion was a widow, and he took me for her husband.

LADY PROUDFOOT. Ah, but lose no time. He must be on the beach now, outside the town. Fly to the fatal spot and avenge me.

PROUDFOOT. Matilda, I fail entirely to gather your meaning.

LADY PROUDFOOT. Of course, I would have permitted no familiarity on his part, but I cannot lie still under the affront he has put upon me. Your wife is compromised.

PROUDFOOT. My wife, like Caesar's, is above suspicion.

LADY PROUDFOOT. No man before has ever trifled with my affections.

PROUDFOOT. My dear, do not excite yourself.

LADY PROUDFOOT. Sebastian, give me his blood.

PROUDFOOT. My love, as you remarked to me before, what would you do with it?

LADY PROUDFOOT. I would wallow in it. (*She does so, in the cushions.*)

PROUDFOOT. I am a man of peace, Matilda. It would be highly indecorous for me to fight a duel. (*Moves to table, L.*)

LADY PROUDFOOT. Do you refuse to cleanse this spot upon my honour?

PROUDFOOT (*turning*). Matilda, the whole subject is distasteful to me. I wish to hear no more about it.

LADY PROUDFOOT. Blood! Sebastian! Blood!

PROUDFOOT. Silence, woman! I tell you I will have no dealings with this foreigner.

LADY PROUDFOOT. Coward! Had I known this before, I would have yielded to his importunity.

E

PROUDFOOT. Matilda, how dare you! How dare you?

> (CAPTAIN CHALFORD *comes in door* U.S. *with swords and a box of pistols.*)

CHALFORD. Do I intrude?

PROUDFOOT. Not at all. On the contrary, we're delighted to see you.

CHALFORD (*moving to table, L., and putting down his arms*). The Countess asked me to come here.

PROUDFOOT. I will tell her that you have arrived.

CHALFORD. Thank you. But before you go, may I ask you to be my second in a little affair I have on my hands?

LADY PROUDFOOT. You don't mean to say that you're going to fight a duel?

CHALFORD. Undoubtedly.

LADY PROUDFOOT. There is a man after my own heart.

PROUDFOOT. And with whom is this desperate encounter?

CHALFORD. Dash my buttons, I don't know. The man tells me he's the Duke of Hermanos.

LADY PROUDFOOT. You are going to kill that Spaniard?

PROUDFOOT (*to his wife*). Who took the Captain for your lover, just as he took me for Marion's husband.

CHALFORD. What on earth do you mean?

> (*Enter* MARION.)

PROUDFOOT (*to* MARION). Ah, you've just come in the nick of time.

MARION (*from* C. S. *to the* CAPTAIN). I'm very cross with you, my friend. You've behaved extremely badly to Lucy.

CHALFORD. Upon my soul, I don't know what I've done.

PROUDFOOT. Listen to me, young man. Why did you become engaged to Lucy, when you were in love with her sister, Marion?

CHALFORD (*astonished*). I?

MARION. The question seems to surprise you, and, upon my word, it could not be put more bluntly. (*Turns and moves over* R. *to* LADY PROUDFOOT.)

LADY PROUDFOOT. The young men of the present day don't seem to know who they're in love with.

CHALFORD. I swear to you on my honour that I have never loved anyone but Lucy. And if I live to be a hundred I shall never love another.

LADY PROUDFOOT. If I'd only married a man like that!

(*Enter* LUCY.)

CHALFORD. Lucy!

LUCY (*coming down* C.). Cruel, cruel Adolphus.

CHALFORD. How could you dream that I loved anyone but you?

MARION. Now run away into the garden and promise one another never to be silly again.

LUCY. Shall we? (*She goes,* L., *to* CHALFORD.)

(*Enter* MARY JANE.)

MARY. The Spanish gentleman is here *again*, ma'am.

PROUDFOOT. Throw him out of the window. Let no mercy be shown him.

CHALFORD. Let me wring his neck for you, shall I?

MARION. On the contrary, let us see him and get rid of him for good and all.

(*Exit* MARY JANE U.S. LUCY *goes out with* CHALFORD L.)

PROUDFOOT (*sitting* L.). That Spaniard is a fool, my dear. Would you believe it, he took me for your husband.

MARION (*from armchair,* D.S.R.). Then it was your ears he boxed?

PROUDFOOT. Oh, it was a mere manner of speaking. I attached no importance to it.

LADY PROUDFOOT. D'you mean to say he dared to touch you, Sebastian?

PROUDFOOT. I flatter myself I had the best of it. I pretended to take no notice.

LADY PROUDFOOT (*to* MARION). We will leave you. (*Rising.*) I will never see him again. Sebastian!

MARION. I think Sir Sebastian had better stay.

PROUDFOOT (*hesitating*). Do you positively insist?

MARION (*smiling*). I won't let him hurt you.

PROUDFOOT. Don't imagine that I fear him.

LADY PROUDFOOT. Sebastian, take no useless risks.

PROUDFOOT. Leave us, defenceless female.

LADY PROUDFOOT (*to* MARION). Take care of him. He has the courage of a lion. When roused he hesitates at nothing. (*Exit through window, L., drawing her shawl about her.* PROUDFOOT *moves to fireplace, R. and the* DUKE *enters, armed.*)

DUKE. Excuse me. It is Captain Chalford that I desire to see.

MARION. Captain Chalford, sir, is with my sister, his betrothed.

DUKE. Then it isn't you he's in love with?

MARION. No, it isn't.

DUKE. *Valgame Dios!* (*Puts arms on table once more.*)

PROUDFOOT (*aside to* MARION). Don't excite him.

MARION (*pointing to* PROUDFOOT). It may also interest you to know that this gentleman is not my husband.

PROUDFOOT (*gallantly*). The loss is mine.

DUKE. Of that fact I am already aware.

MARION. Then perhaps you will be so good as not to inflict yourself upon us again!

DUKE. Do you wish me to go?

PROUDFOOT. It looks suspiciously like it.

DUKE. I cannot. I have had too much trouble to get here. I shall not go till I have seen your husband.

PROUDFOOT. But the lady's husband is . . .

MARION (*aside to* PROUDFOOT). Ssh! (*She goes to* DUKE c.) Do you positively insist on seeing my husband?

DUKE. Positively.

MARION. Then—you may wait for him.

DUKE. Where is he?

MARION. Travelling.

DUKE. When will he return?

MARION. I have no idea.

DUKE. I will certainly wait.

MARION. He may be quite a while, you know.

DUKE. I have all the time, thank you.

MARION. I think I should tell you that he's gone a long way.

DUKE. Every journey has an ending.

PROUDFOOT (*aside*). Not that one.

MARION. As you will. (*Curtsies.*) Sir. I've certainly seen plainer men.

> (*Exit* PROUDFOOT L. MARION *stops for a moment to look at* DUKE *and drops her handkerchief.*)

DUKE. You have dropped your handkerchief.

MARION. I have. (*Exit.*)

DUKE. If I wait ten years, I will see that husband.

> (*Enter* COUNT U.S.)

COUNT. Here I am at last. (*Seeing the* DUKE.) *Tiens!*

DUKE (*aside*). Who the devil is this?

COUNT (*putting parcels on couch*). Excuse my agitation. I feared I was late. I've been quite a journey.

DUKE. I wonder if this is the husband, by any chance. (*Walking in front of* COUNT *and eyeing him.*) Have you, indeed?

COUNT. What for does he prance round me?

DUKE. This time I will be very cautious. Once bit, twice shy!

COUNT. There must be something very odd about me. Pardon me, have I ze smut on my nose?

DUKE. So you have been travelling!

COUNT (*rather surprised*). I have.

DUKE. Ha, ha! I am grow warm. Have you been far?

COUNT. Don't speak of it!

DUKE. I am growing hot. Have you been a journey?

COUNT. I seem to have been to the world's end.

DUKE. I burn! I positively burn! And what are those parcels?

COUNT. They're only some things I've brought back for my wife.

DUKE. Since you speak of your wife, you are obviously married.

COUNT. I am; but I really don't see that it is any business of yours.

DUKE (*shaking hands effusively*). My dear fellow, I'm delighted to meet you!

COUNT. It's very pleasant to hear you say so.

DUKE. I've been wanting to see you all day.

COUNT. Whom have I the great pleasure of addressing?

DUKE. Don Ferdinand Francisco Maria de Lomas y Oria, Duke of Hermanos.

COUNT. And how can I be of service to you?

DUKE. I do not like your face.

COUNT. I do not like it very much myself.

DUKE. I have reason to believe that your maternal grandmother was no better than she should be.

COUNT. I have always suspected it. Tell me, was it the coachman or was it the dancing-master?

DUKE. Your waistcoat is unpardonably loud.

COUNT. You are offensive, sir. You may say what you like of my face and you may say what you like about my maternal grandmother but I will allow no man to question my taste in waistcoats.

DUKE. I declare and I repeat that I strongly object to your waistcoat and I insist on your immediately removing it.

COUNT. Do you know, sir, that men have died for less than this?

DUKE. In point of fact I have come here to challenge you to mortal combat.

COUNT. Why on earth didn't you say so. I shall be delighted to oblige you. Will the beach suit you outside the town?

DUKE. Perfectly. Have you any choice of weapons? I have here swords and pistols.

COUNT. I leave it entirely to you.

DUKE. I advise you forthwith to commend your soul to Providence. I am an unerring shot and the best swordsman in Europe.

COUNT. Look to your pistols, sir, and leave my soul to look after itself.

DUKE (*bowing*). Sir.

COUNT (*bowing*). Sir. As a mere matter of curiosity would you oblige me by telling me why you come here to challenge me to a duel. To the best of my belief you had not then seen my waistcoat.

DUKE. Sir, in Spain when we love a woman we are ready to fight the whole world in order to gain her. I love your wife.

COUNT. You don't.

DUKE. I have sworn that she shall be mine.

COUNT. My dear fellow, I have been looking for you for years.

DUKE. Me?

COUNT. Take her, dear boy. I will not stand in your way. It's quite unnecessary that we should fight on that account. Withdraw your highly offensive objection to my waistcoat and she is yours.

DUKE. Do I understand that you are willing to surrender her.

COUNT. Lock, stock and barrel. Does she love you?

DUKE. To distraction.

COUNT. Then all is for the best in the best of all possible worlds, but don't waste time, women are fickle and apt to change their minds.

DUKE. I have post-horses round the corner.

COUNT. Swear to me that you will make her happy.

DUKE. I will make her happy as the day is long.

COUNT. You are a total stranger to me, but you are a good friend; I shall not forget the kindness you have shown me.

DUKE. I confess that your eagerness to get rid of your wife takes me somewhat by surprise.

COUNT. She is the best woman in the world; she is good, she is beautiful, she is virtuous; do not hesitate to take her. It's a chance in a thousand, but be quick about it on account of the horses.

DUKE. Your wife will need a little time to pack.

COUNT. I will help her; I'm a very quick packer.

DUKE. You certainly are.

> (COUNTESS *heard talking, off.*)

COUNT. Here she is, we will break the glad tidings to her at once.

> (*Enter* COUNTESS *from windows,* L.)

COUNTESS (*to* DUKE). You here again.

COUNT. Never to leave your side, my angel. This gentleman has told me your secret. My only wish in life is to make you happy. He loves you, you love him, I stand aside.

COUNTESS. What nonsense are you talking now?

DUKE. That is not your wife?

COUNT. That most surely is my wife.

DUKE. Then it is not the lady I am going to run away with.

COUNT. Let us have no trifling. Did you tell me that you were in love with my wife or not?

DUKE. I did.

COUNT. And did you not say that you would hesitate at nothing to get her?

DUKE. I did.

COUNT. Well, there she is, take her.

DUKE. I will not take her.

COUNT. You shall take her; I will allow no one to play fast and loose with the affections of my wife.

DUKE. But that isn't the wife I meant.

COUNT. That is the only wife I have.

DUKE. I can't help that, but that's no affair of mine.

COUNT. I do not like your face, sir.

DUKE. I do.

COUNT. Your maternal grandmother was no better than she should be.

DUKE. But with a king.

COUNT. I do not like your waistcoat either.

DUKE. Then I can only deplore your taste. I am the best dressed man in Europe, sir. I wish you a very good day.

COUNT. You shall leave this room only over my dead body.

DUKE. I tell you this is not the wife I meant.

COUNT. Come, come, sir, this is idle talk. Are you prepared to fulfil your obligations or must I force you to behave like a gentleman at the end of a rapier?

DUKE. I am prepared to give you satisfaction where and when you choose but I will not elope with a perfect stranger.

COUNTESS. If you'll only let me get a word in, I think I can explain the mistake.

COUNT. I am not in a humour to listen to an explanation. This fellow has grievously insulted you and it is my duty to avenge you.

COUNTESS. Wait a minute, I think I know what to do. (*Exit quickly*, U.S.)

DUKE. I am willing to admit for the first time in my life that I have made a mistake.

COUNT. You certainly have if you thought you could trifle with the honour of a French nobleman.

DUKE. Are you a French nobleman?

COUNT. Count de Moret. No unworthy antagonist for the Duke of Hermanos, I flatter myself.

DUKE. I took you for Mr. Nairne.

COUNT. I do not care who you took me for. Unless you are prepared to elope with my wife within fifteen minutes I insist on satisfaction.

DUKE. Sir, I am a grandee of Spain with the right to wear my hat in the presence of the King, and I brook insult from no man. I will meet you on the beach outside the town in one hour.

COUNT. I do not intend to let you out of my sight. It has not escaped my memory that you have post-horses waiting round the corner.

DUKE. Are you suspecting me of wishing to avoid the encounter?

COUNT. Yes, sir. I think you are a coward, otherwise you would not be afraid to run away with my wife.

DUKE. This is too much. (*Springing* U.S. *to table,* L.) Here are weapons. Do you choose swords or pistols? (*Brandishes pistols.*)

COUNT. Pistols are too noisy. The sword is the only weapon that befits a gentleman.

DUKE. You are a man after my own heart. I took quite a fancy to you the first moment I saw you.

COUNT. Do not think I dislike you, I couldn't have wished my wife's second husband to be a more delightful fellow.

DUKE. The choice is yours. (*Holding out foils.*)

    (*Enter* MARION, COUNTESS, LADY PROUDFOOT *and* PROUDFOOT *through doors,* U.S.)

MARION. Stop!

    (LADY PROUDFOOT *screams and faints into* PROUDFOOT's *arms.* MARION *has moved to* DUKE, C.)

DUKE. Marion.

MARION. What is the meaning of this?

DUKE. I thought the gentleman was your husband and I was preparing to kill him. It appears he isn't your husband, but he wants me to kill him all the same.

MARION. Nonsense.

DUKE. He insists on it.

COUNT (*declaiming from fireplace*). He has insulted my wife by refusing to elope with her.

PROUDFOOT. This is what comes of spending summer on the Continent. (*He takes* LADY PROUDFOOT *to the sofa, as she recovers.* CHALFORD *and* LUCY *appear at the windows,* L.)

COUNTESS (*moving* D.S.R., *to the* COUNT). I am sorry to disappoint you, my dear, but it's not me the Duke wants to run away with, but Marion.

COUNT (*shouting excitably*). Why the devil didn't he say so at once? Really, sir, your conduct is inexcusable.

DUKE (*slanging back across room*). Do me the justice to admit that I have not tried to excuse it.

MARION. Be quiet!

DUKE (c.s. *with* MARION). Where is your husband?

MARION. My husband is dead.

DUKE. Dead! The devil take me!

MARION. I hope he won't or you'll meet my husband at last.

DUKE. But, if you are a widow, what obstacle is there to your marrying me?

MARION. None, that I know of.

DUKE. Then you will marry me?

MARION. No!

DUKE. No? No? I never take no for an answer.

MARION. Never?

DUKE. Never!

MARION. Then there is only one other thing that I can say.

DUKE. And what's that?

> (MARION *takes nosegay from table and throws it through the window.* CHALFORD *and* LUCY *duck.*)

Yes!

> (*General murmur from all.*)

Ah, madam, how you have had the laugh of me. I must wait for your husband. They think I am the disappointed and all the time I am the appointed.

COUNT. Then there is no need to fight a duel?

PROUDFOOT. None whatever.

CHALFORD. How distressing.

DUKE. I liked you from the first; we were born to be brothers-in-law.

CHALFORD. Really!

MARION. And this is Lady Proudfoot.

> (LADY PROUDFOOT *inclines.*)

DUKE. It is fortunate that my heart was engaged when first I fixed you with my glance.

MARION. And this is Sir Sebastian Proudfoot.

DUKE. Sir, I should vastly have regretted your early death.

(PROUDFOOT *bows.* MARY JANE *enters.*)

MARY. Supper is served, my lady.

(*Exeunt in pairs, chatting gaily*—LADY PROUDFOOT *and the* COUNT, PROUDFOOT *and the* COUNTESS, CHALFORD *and* LUCY, *arm-in-arm and hand-in-hand.* MARION, *who has moved over to windows* L., *remains with the* DUKE.)

MARION (*in the moonlight*). Sir, will you give me your arm?

(DUKE *goes to* MARION *and kisses her.* MARY JANE *closes the doors, smiling and peeping.*)

CURTAIN

# PROPERTY PLOT

## Act I (*Morning*)

**SET**

Round, folding table set for breakfast with coffee, milk, lump sugar, rolls, butter, napkins, cups and saucers, plates, knives, spoons, etc., newspaper.

Sofa.

Occasional table, tapestry on it.

One or two armchairs.

Four dining-room chairs.

Flowers in vases.

Smelling salts in bottle on mantelpiece.

Bell pull by fireplace.

Other furniture *ad lib.*

**PERSONAL (*Off*)**

Shrimping net ⎫
Boots       ⎬ PROUDFOOT
Hat         ⎭

Hat and gloves—DUKE

Flower (in her dress)—MARION

Shoes and stocking—
          LADY PROUDFOOT

## Act II (*Afternoon*)

**STRIKE**

Breakfast things; fold down table flap.

**SET**

Tapestry on table by sofa.

**PERSONAL**

A marguerite—LADY PROUDFOOT.

**PERSONAL (*off*)**

Bouquet of flowers—MARY JANE
Shawl—LUCY.
Hat—PROUDFOOT.

## Act III (*Evening*)

**SET**

Lamps on; bouquet in vase on table.

**PERSONAL**

Book—LUCY.
Shawl—LADY PROUDFOOT.
Handkerchief—MARION.

**PERSONAL (*off*)**

Brandy—MARY JANE.
Foils and case of pistols—DUKE.
Swords and box of pistols—CAPT CHALFORD.

Lightning Source UK Ltd.
Milton Keynes UK
UKOW06f2358250416

272970UK00001B/94/P